On Becoming

NaughtABimbeaux™

The Smart Woman's Guide
to Finding Her
PRINCE
Without
Ever
Kissing
Another
Frog

Morgan Rose, M.S.

Book and Cover Copyrights © 2013 by Morgan Rose

Cover design: Morgan Rose

First printing: May 2013

PUBLISHING CATALOGING-IN-PUBLICATION DATA

Rose, Morgan

On Becoming NaughtABimbeaux ~ The Smart Woman's Guide to Finding Her Prince Without Ever Kissing Another Frog /

Morgan Rose, M.S.

ISBN 978-0-988-8800-0-9

i

Ms. Rose gratefully acknowledges all the writers she has quoted from for their wisdom and inspiration. An exhaustive search was done to determine whether previously published material in this book required permission to reprint. If any author was not appropriately recognized, the author apologizes, and with notification, that material will be credited in subsequent editions.

Special Thank You: Red Hen Press, Bart Baggett, and United States Centers for Disease Control and Prevention.

DEDICATION

To Daddy who from the day of my birth
lifted me up with his laughter and love
and set my course for life.
I miss you.

And to the Single Sisterhood, I hope this book fulfills
the promise of your value and vision
for having what you want for your life.

INVITATION

"It's in every one of us to be wise.
Find your heart, open up both your eyes.
We can all know everything, without ever knowing why.
It's in every one of us, by and by."
David Pomeranz

INSPIRATION

"Some women wait for something to change
and nothing does change, so they change themselves."
Audre Lorde

ACKNOWLEDGMENTS

I am blest with a lifetime of tried and true soul sisters who have loved me through the good times and the not so good times. Joanne "Rosey," Lindsell Webber, my Rose Queen competitor and friend since before we will admit; Betty Mac ~ my best high school friend, drill team partner, UCLA roomie, and bridesmaid; Juliah Jayne Jensen ~ my "retread' and beyond loyal friend, for both your support of me and the America's Angel Campaign, and your sacred sense that I must finish this book; Izabella Dante "Izzy" Janssen ~ my adorable Goddess run amok, thank you for listening always; Kaer Soutthard ~ forever faithful, loving and competent friend, without you where would the America's Angel Campaign be; Miranda Goll ~ you are wise beyond your years, and have kept the Campaign on course while I've been writing like a mad woman; Lois Mikawa ~ for your faithfulness and hilarious sense of humor during an extraordinarily difficult time and beyond ~ be well, my dear friend; Karen Rae Wilson ~ your gifts for expressing the wisdom of women, and for uplifting my life have made all the difference; and to my dear friends: Lisa Shapiro and Patti Kerr, my Grant Gang, Sandy Rifkin, Linda Rose, and my fabulous colleagues and friends, Marta Carrasco and Judith Adams…thanks for all the hilarity and understanding when I disappeared into my computer cave for months at a time. Thank you to my clients, who for over many years, and many tears, your courage has strengthened mine. Thanks to each one of you from my whole heart.

I want to thank Amanita Rosenbush, my book's first editor who, though a task-master, taught me to think about the power of my written words more than anyone before or after. A special shout-out to Anne Lamott ~ Author Extraordinaire. Anne, though we've never met, your thoughts on writing from the heart have kept me keeping on writing what I feel more than what I think.

Thank you to my soul-brother, Jim Sporleter, Principal of Lincoln High School in Walla Walla, Washington, who is raising the national bar for compassionate education. Thank you for saying "Yes," to my invitation to join the Board of Directors of the America's Angel Campaign. You are, indeed, ~ as a husband, father, grandfather, leader of children and those who teach them ~ a true Prince Charming.

Thank you to my niece, Tricia, who is such a friend of my heart and one of the truly wise ones, for you knew to ask the question, *Is he WORTHY of Me?* when you met and tested your Prince Charming, Matthew. Together, your love ensures that Pierce will grow into a Prince like his daddy, and Teagan will know her Prince when she finds him, just like her Momma did.

And, with special and very deep love to my sons David, Jonathan, and Adam, and daughter-in law, Jenna, and most of all my grand baby girls Caroline and Lucy Joy… even thinking of how much I love you makes my eyes all misty.

CONTENTS

Dedication iii

Acknowledgements v

Introduction ix

PART I ~ ME

The Challenge to Cherish You 1

1. Bimbo Meets *NaughtABimbeaux:*
   Defining Our Terms 3

2. What are You Pretending Naught to Know?:
   Excavating Your Truth 15

3. Once Upon a Lifetime: *Lasting Impressions*
   of Your 1st Prince Charming 25

4. "Shoulding" On Your Life?: *Confronting the*
   "Celestial Should Committee" Myth 53

5. Into Your Intuition: *When in Doubt,*
   Trust Your Tummy 63

6. The Choice Is Always Yours: *A Parable of Power* 69

7. The Power of Your Words: *She-Brain at the Ready* 73

8. Sisterhood: *Holding You UP When You're*
   Falling Down 81

9. Tassels: *The POWER of Alphabet Soup ~*
   It's Academic, Girlfiend 91

10. Cinderella Revisited: *aka CinderFella ~*
    It's ALL About the Slipper 99

11. Mirror, Mirror On The Wall,
    He Might First See You at the Mall 109

12. On A Clear Day You Can See Who You Are 127

PART II ~ The BRIDGE

From Woman to the World Beyond **139**

13 Biology of Bonding:
   Neuropsychobiology for Dummies 141

14 Analyze This! *Reading the Handwriting on the Wall,
   or Maybe Just on a Nice Cocktail Napkin* 151

PART III ~ HE

The Relevance of Research When Choosing One's Prince **161**

15 I Finally Got It: *Men Don't Get It
   & That's Just the Way It Is* 163

16 Mr. Right vs. Mr. Right Now:
   The Joy of Mediocrity 171

17 Mr. Right vs. Mr. I'll Be Right Back:
   The Joy of Commitment-Phobia............................179

18 Mr. Right vs. Mr. Always Right:
   The Joy of Narcissism, aka "King Me" 187

19 Little Boy Blue:
   The Vulnerability of Grownup Little Boys 205

PART IV ~ WE

Whatever Souls are Made of, Yours and

Mine are the Same...**215**

20 Anam Cara: *The Truest Friend of Your Soul*..................217

About the Author **229**

Bread for the Journey.......................................**233**

INTRODUCTION

From the time I heard my first love story,
I started looking for you.

Rumi

This was supposed to be easy, right? Once you grew up, there would magically appear the man of your dreams, casting you that stunning first glance across the crowded room, and folding hand into hand, and heart into heart, you would stroll as one through the envying crowd, together forever into eternal bliss. Your handsome prince would _____, and _____, and _____ your every need, and you would, indeed, live happily ever after. Never, never was there anything about kissing frogs.

For those of us in the Single Sisterhood, looking for *Mr. Right* is as unconscious as breathing. Whether we are new to the game, or well-seasoned survivors, when we are sweating at the gym, sipping cappuccinos at Starbucks, stopped at the red light, or making strained conversation on the first ~ and last ~ date with *Mr. Wrong*, we females silently scan the space we're in, searching for that one perfect specimen who catches our eye. When we actually spy such a stunning one, and those bright sparks fly, our wishful heart tramples all sense of logic as we charge forth into a primal rush to *Fantasyland*, with our little girl illusions of ... *and they all lived happily ever after*. Never mind trying to change this. It's a survival thing.

In Neanderthal times, the relationship bar was set pretty low for females who needed only to ensure protection for themselves and their offspring. As you are likely well aware, our relationship bar is set quite a bit higher. Unlike our Neanderthal sisters, when considering your potential mate, your evolved brain is capable of more complex priorities than simply assessing body mass and ability to hunt to kill anything that moves. Ironically, in either era, female observes male. The difference is that for Cave Girl Cate, dating and mating pretty much involved *What you see is what you get.* End of story.

For you, what you see is a mere smidgeon of what you might get if you leap before you really look. So, if you are still depending on Cate's unconscious and impulsive approach to dating, the *happily ever after* ending is a rare, if ever, outcome. Maybe you're OK with investing precious time as your biological clock tick tocks through a never ending saga of ticking time bombs, or just some harmless cuckoos, setting yourself up to repeat, ad nauseum, the ***But he's so nice / cute / rich / available*** dead end. Maybe you get a rush charging head first into another brick wall, only to discover, once again, that you've wasted your time and tears on a man who offers you no future. I call this the *Pasta Principle*, because you've convinced yourself that if you just throw enough spaghetti on the wall, surely one of them will stick. But, if a slightly more enlightened approach interests you, read on.

Before you risk getting burned again boiling any more pasta, would it be worth a bit of your time to turn off the stove (i.e., take a time-out from mindless dating), and, instead take a time-in to open your mind and learn what you need to know to have what you want?

> ***There is more hunger for love***
> ***in this world than for bread.***
> Mother Teresa

If what you are looking for is love that lasts a lifetime, learning how to open your mind's eye to see below the surface would be a good thing. Thankfully, it's also not difficult. That is, if you are willing to shift from the prehistoric approach of *I see male, I grab male* to *I see that male, and I will watch him for a while **to see if he is worthy of me**.* Why? Because how he looks doesn't guarantee how he loves. And, how he loves you is the ultimate question.

So, if your story falls a bit short, and maybe reads more like *Tales from the Crypt* than *Cinderella*, maybe it's time to turn *Once upon a Time* into Real Life. What if you could predict if that man eying you across the crowded room, or rumpled up in your sheets, or just coming around that next corner was your longed for prince? What value would you place on knowing, *Is he fraud?* or *Is he Forever?* before you hand over your heart to his keeping?

> **One good man, one good man, it ain't much**
> **~ it's only everything.**
> Deborah Kerr

If you are seeking yet another quick fix for solving the heart wrenching state of your love life, then *On Becoming NaughtABimbeaux* is probably not the book for you.

But, if you:

Have done all the right things to make him happy, make him comfortable, make him **stay** only to watch his back as he walks, runs, sneaks out of your life

Have loved with wild abandon, then found yourself abandoned

Have valued being in a relationship more than you have valued yourself

Have lost your sense of self by giving in to his

Have wondered what you are missing in how to play the game of love

Have thought you could not survive another wrenching affair

Are ready to take control and insist on what you deserve in life and love

Are committed to finding the one extraordinary someone who will fill your bed, your body, your heart, your mind and your future with joy…then what is offered here will support you.

> *Little girls know they are lovable*
> *because big people love them.*
> *Big girls know they are lovable*
> *because they love themselves.*
> *It's all a matter of perspective.*

Morgan Rose

A Word about Your Journey

In the book you hold in your hand is a journey of twenty chapters between you and your heart's desire. Within these pages you will find respect for your integrity, intelligence and vulnerability. The emotional upheaval you have somehow managed to survive will be held with compassion and dignity. Your commitment to live an empowered life and find authentic love will be supported every step of your way.

The book is arranged in four strategic sections that guide you step-by-step out of your dead-end relationship maze and towards the holy grail of authentic love. On your way, you will learn the real dynamics of having and holding love for a lifetime.

Part I   ME: A Journey into Personal Healing, Discovery, and Authenticity

From this place of strength you cross…

Part II   The BRIDGE: Acquiring Tools Worth a King's Ransom for Discerning the Worthiness of a Potential Prince

From this place of empowerment you consider…

Part III   HE: The Relevance of Research when Choosing Your Prince

From this place of wisdom you will know if HE and ME are meant to be…

Part IV   WE: ANAM CARA: *Whatever Souls Are Made Of, Yours and Mine are the Same*   Emily Bronte

Each chapter engages your intellect, intuition, imagination, emotions and hopes to inspire a consciousness shift. When supportive of a particular chapter's focus, research from the science of human intimacy connects the dots so you can make sense of the nonsense of your past relationships. Chapter themes clarify who you are as a woman, the qualities that define your prince, and how to lead with your head and save your heart for when you are absolutely sure you have found him. This process requires a bit more than finding a new shade of lipstick, hiking one's hemline, or cultivating a compulsion for NFL stats. It requires you to open the door to your soul and embrace all you discover there. When you do, the question *Will he like me?* will shift to **Is he WORTHY of Me?** and nothing will ever be the same, again.

Throughout the chapters you will learn the answers to:

- How do I tell which men can and which men can't love, before I hand over my heart?

- Why do I so often love the men who can't?

- What makes some men lay, lie, then leave?

- Why does settling feel like I've sold out my soul?

- Is it really that important to love myself first?

- Why do my daddy and his mommy matter?

- What's science got to do with it?

This journey about to unfold within you is uniquely yours. It will require great courage for it will transform all you believe about love. It will open your eyes, change your perspective and break through whatever has been holding you back from having the love you want. Each step leads you to first value *yourself* before searching for that one person who will value you above all others, because loving yourself is the key to everything else.

As in any journey, simply having the map does not ensure that you will reach your destination. Rather, your success depends 100% on the honesty, commitment, and courage you bring to every step of the way. I encourage you to give yourself time to discover the treasure hidden in each chapter before you move on to the next, because learning how to live a conscious life takes time.

Every chapter begins by defining the terms that highlight the subject of that chapter. Following **Our Terms** will be stories from our shared sisterhood that give you examples of the chapter theme. At the end of each chapter you will find prompts for your **Journey Journaling** and **Mirror Magic** exercises to enlighten and empower you. The time you give to these exercises will make all the difference. **Recommended Reads** are books that have been client-tested over time. Each recommended book is intended to expand on the chapter's lesson if you desire to learn more about that particular step in your journey.

The only guarantee for your journey is that when you commit with all your heart, soul and mind you will change your life. So, take your time, do your work, feel your pain, conquer your dragons, journal your truth, laugh at what's funny, cry at what's sad, and first, last and always… love you. When you reach the end, you will have what you came here to find. You will realize that you already hold within you the woman you want to be to have the man you want to hold. Most importantly, you will stand at the center of your universe knowing all you need to solve the mystery of having and holding authentic love as a woman in the 21st Century.

> *Not I, nor anyone else can travel this road for you.*
> *You must travel it by yourself. It is not far.*
> *It is within reach. Perhaps you have been on it*
> *since you were born, and did not know.*
> Walt Whitman

JOURNEY JOURNAL:

Journaling is key to your journey. All you will need is a notebook or journal and a pen. The **power** of journaling comes from within you. When you write your thoughts, memories, hopes and dreams, you bring your truth forward, out of your sub-conscious mind onto the page and into your life. The act of writing them down on paper strengthens your resolve to make them real. Another important bonus: Research has proven that journaling benefits our physical and mental health.

MIRROR MAGIC:

This is one of the most empowering exercises I recommend to my clients. It is powerful in its simplicity and potential to heal your hurts.

Stand in front of your mirror, look straight into your eyes, then simply, honestly repeat *I love you.* Even in a matter of seconds, this most personal act of soul intimacy can move you to that deep place within. Variations of the **Mirror Magic** message are included at the end of each of the first twelve chapters. You can also feel free to make up your own. To be most effective, the phrase is best repeated several times. Be prepared for tears.

BREAD for the JOURNEY:

At the end of the book you will find a list of additional resources to support your journey. I encourage you to try some of these suggestions as they have proven to be valuable resources for many of our sisters to move forward in their lives.

On Becoming NaughtABimbeaux

PART I

ME

The Challenge to Cherish You

1 *Bimbo Meets NaughtABimbeaux:* Defining Our Terms

*It's really fun to act like a bimbo. But it's fun to act like a bimbo
only when people know that you really aren't.*
Laura Dern

*She threw herself eagerly into the paths
of unsuitable men.*
Anne Taintor

*If you put a small value upon yourself,
rest assured that the world will not raise your price.*
Anonymous

Our Terms:

Where your love life has been...

Bim/bộ as defined in Webster's Dictionary (yes, it really is there!):
A foolish, stupid, or inept person; an attractive but stupid young woman,
especially one with loose morals; person who lacks sense, forethought,
caution, ordinary quickness and keenness of mind; tediously dull person.

Where you want to be...

NaughtABimbeaux (not a bim/bộ) is defined:

ENLIGHTENED: To be free of ignorance and false beliefs.

WISE: Having discernment; judging properly what is true.

POWERFUL: Possessing great authority, or influence.

DISCERNING: The ability to make wise, personal decisions.

KATHLEEN

If there was such a thing as Bimbos Anonymous, Kathleen would have been the group's poster child. About to celebrate her fiftieth birthday, no one who knew Kathleen would disagree. Kathleen approached finding a meaningful relationship using the *Pasta Principle*. She truly believed that if she just threw enough spaghetti at the wall, surely one of them would stick. So, with vigor, she pursued quantity in hopes of finding quality. Her family and circle of friends had witnessed one episode after another of her short-lived, unwise, and doomed to fail romances. It was as if her heart was a revolving door, and every time a man exited she would cry as if her heart had broken, then say *Next*.

Kathleen was short, blonde, friendly and hysterically funny. She was, also, independently wealthy and frighteningly naïve. To be truthful, Kathleen was a little girl in a woman's body, and nothing anyone had said or would say was going to change her! So, her daughters and friends protected her as best they could from unsuitable suitors.

Kathleen met men through the Internet, at dances, and at downtown and uptown bars. This little bimbo believed that if she was nice to a man he would be nice to her, and so she was nice to every man she met. Men read her openness and charm as an easy conquest, so it was a rare evening when the promise of new romance wasn't in the air. It was obvious to everyone else that such blind trust hid her terror of growing old, alone.

No matter where she met a man, Kathleen remained true to her strict English upbringing. The proper way for a man to court a lady was to call for her at her home. This rule only compounded Kathleen's problem, for once a man drove up her winding driveway and scanned the front of her mansion, his hope of sexual conquest instantly ran a distant second to the potential of her fortune. As each cad placed his greedy finger on the doorbell, one could almost hear *Eureka* harmonizing with those lovely brass chimes echoing down through the valley below.

Kathleen met Allen through a personal ad, and after one date she was head over heels! She assured her daughters and her friends that this one was promising. Besides being *nice* (aren't they all in the beginning?), Allen had a college education and owned his own business. Sounding too good to be true, her friends arranged a dinner party to check Allen, *the nice guy*, out. Kathleen's friends insisted that Allen would be politely ushered out the door at the end of the evening, leaving them to share their honest impressions with her.

Consensus: Allen did seem normal, certainly more normal than the others, and so they gave their cautious blessing. The whirlwind romance was ON! Three weeks later, Allen invited Kathleen to spend a weekend with him at a new golfing resort about three hours away. Of course, she accepted. When they returned, Kathleen could hardly contain herself. She invited her daughters and best friends for lunch, saying only that she had very important news.

Before the soup was even served, she blurted out, ***He loves me!! He really loves me!!!*** Lois, the friend who had known Kathleen the longest and felt most responsible for her, asked the obvious question: *Kathleen, how do you know he loves you? How could you possibly know this soon that he truly loves you?*

As tears streamed down her face and everyone held their breath, Kathleen's story tumbled out. She and Allen had enjoyed a lovely drive up to the resort. He even seemed a bit more attentive than usual, touching her arm and squeezing her hand as they drove. They shared lunch in the Club's beautiful dining room, looking out at the panoramic view of the 18th hole and the mountains beyond. Allen ordered a well-chilled bottle of Dom Perignon and then toasted Kathleen with the words, *I love you*. She hardly ate a bite of her lunch.

As if on cue, just as the plates had been cleared, a man approached their table. He introduced himself as the agent for the new luxury subdivision being built around the golf course. When he explained to Kathleen that Allen had called him two weeks ago about purchasing a lot, she thought her heart was going to burst! She had no idea that Allen was already so sure of his love that he was planning to share his life with her. They spent the weekend looking at lots and planning their dream home together. Kathleen had no memory of her feet ever touching the ground.

As everyone listened to this all too predictable story, Lois, again, took the plunge as she asked, *Kathleen, but how do you know he loves you?* Kathleen's frustration sounded loud and clear as she shouted, **Didn't you hear me? He told me he loved me!** Desperate to open the eyes of her dearest friend, Lois fired back, *Oh yes, we all heard that. But how many men have told you they love you, Kathleen? Words are cheap. So, there must be something else, and we are all ears to hear what it is!* Kathleen took a deep breath, then a smile came across her face as she answered, *Because he wants to meet my CPA! No man has ever wanted that before!* Lois took the hand of her friend, looked into her eyes and said, *Oh, darling Kathleen, can't you see you are too delirious with the idea of love to understand your story makes us suspicious that it's only your money Allen wants?*

When it hurts more to suffer than to change, you will change.
Author Unknown

Kathleen's understanding of love had failed to mature with her years. As a woman, every new romance recycled the naïve hopes that hid in every one of her childhood crushes. Remember your first? Was it in the rush of those going steady, breaking up, making up, making out, feeling crazy, feeling high, boy crazy high school days? Your yearbook featured photos of Friday night football, but everyone knew the real game in town was played, perhaps scored, in the backseat of a car far away from stadium lights and referees calling *foul.*

It didn't much matter if you watched from the sidelines or played full body contact. There was no denying your body was now captive to a sophisticated cocktail of hormones and pheromones and that exotic beckoning door of the unknown. Even men were dizzy with your power! OK, fuzzy-chinned boys, but there was no denying it was a time of heretofore unimagined flirtation! Your emotions ran the gamut from intoxicated, obsessed, fearful, tearful and just plain dizzy with this sudden power of the feminine.

Racing the wind straight into your life, and oblivious to what may come, you handed your heart over to one adolescent male after another. In time, if you didn't beat him to it, he would break your heart without breaking a sweat.

Later, seeking refuge behind your locker door, you cried your tears, swore your shattered heart would never recover, then BOOM! some new baby face ~ with a slightly more chiseled peach-fuzz chin ~ would smile in your direction and you rebounded quicker than Michael Jordan. It was OK. You were growing up. It was all you had imagined and oh! so much more! Not for one moment did doubt dance across your mind that all this juiciness was leading you to your one true love. As sure as the morning dawn, he was waiting for you somewhere just beyond tomorrow and the novice *Game of Love* would soon be called due to the real thing.

When I was a child I spoke as a child, I understood as a child, I thought as a child. But when I became a take care of it myself because there is no one else to do it for me, on my own, doing just fine, thank you very much, grown up woman, I put away childish things.
1 Corinthians 13:11, paraphrased.

From all appearances, you are doing fine ~ at least that's what you tell yourself, your friends, and your increasingly concerned relatives. You have created a life that scores somewhere between somewhat satisfying to ravenously successful. You have enough intelligence to pass your classes, earn your degree, land a job, launch a career, budget your finances, plan for your future, choose great friends, and if necessary, start over again and again.

Your family supports you, and if not, you create one that does. When the unexpected catastrophe interrupts the flow of your routine, you manage to tunnel through, over or around, learn a few lessons and get on with it. It is fair to say that you are a capable adult who accepts responsibility, takes pride in your accomplishments, makes rational decisions, is trustworthy, honors your friendships, and is in control of your life…

Well, maybe not all of your life. The final chapter in your Book of Love remains in draft form with so many erasures it is frightening to see the similarities to your first high school essay. Even the saga of your search for that one kind, nurturing, gallant, lusty, fulfilling and adorable prince reads like your high school diary. But Bimbo? Surely not! You are nowhere near Debbie Does Dallas. So, how do you explain that your journey towards lasting love has run so far amok?

> **Sometimes I lie awake at night and I ask,**
> **'Where have I gone wrong?' Then a voice says to me,**
> **'This is going to take more than one night.'**
> Charlie Brown

In rare private moments that nagging question reminds you he is not here. On occasion, you dare to look that question straight in the eye as you think back to when your young heart played at love. You never imagined being here, now, living a single life with your woman's heart still longing to love and be loved. So, determined, you try, yet again, this time, as in the last time, in earnest. Out come your self-help books like *How to Seduce, Connive, Manipulate, Coerce, Placate, Everything Just Short of Sedating Some Poor Unsuspecting Fellow into Meeting You at the Altar, or At Least Asking You Out in Thirty Days or Less.*

You join a gym. Maybe you even go. The magazine pile on your nightstand grows faster than Jack's beanstalk as you scavenge the pages to learn the latest fashions for your figure, hair styles for your face, how to lose ten pounds in as many days, and devour the featured article: *The 10 Best Ways to Turn Him On and Why He's Not Telling.*

Finally, looking as casual as Jolie at the Oscar's, you nonchalantly set yourself in the midst of your local Happy Hour, politely ignoring all your former **I mean it this time** promises that you were NEVER doing the bar scene again. Then, lo and behold, a potential prince walks your way. Next, with moves as smooth as James Bond, he conveniently slides in beside you and you are off to the races. Your impression? *Nice,* as in a pleasant enough face, can carry on a coherent conversation, smiles at your attempts at wit, and, mission accomplished, gets around to asking you out for a date.

Next step: Close eyes, open heart with blind trust that what you see is what you get. You've known him less than an hour as you begin planning your future together. Why? Because when a potential prince appears, the countdown to happily ever after starts NOW! (Notice any similarities to your scenario and our friend, Kathleen, or Neanderthal Cate the Cave Girl?)

OK, so after an hour, or twenty-four, or even a few months, your prince morphs into frog. Do you cut your losses and move on? Do you try the old Pygmalion ploy by changing him into the man who could be Prince? OK, so perhaps he isn't into personal change. Next option: If he doesn't bolt first, you can always map out your hasty retreat. You know the drill.

> **Insanity is doing the same thing over and over,**
> **and each time expecting a different result.**
> Albert Einstein

After each doomed episode finding out that Mr. Right is really Mr. Wrong, there's a strong possibility you end up in tears. Your friends cast you their knowing looks, then loan you books on how to survive the latest emotional wrenching of your broken heart. With titles such as

Just Get Rid of Him, you know you must have missed something along the way. But what? Perhaps the bigger question is, *Why is it that your adult love life never manages to graduate from high school?*

> **It takes courage to grow up and become who you really are.**
> E. E. Cummings

Your longing for love is legitimate, however, your commitment to finding your phantom prince without kissing any more frogs, you now realize, is not child's play. Games, manipulations, and wishful thinking are the fairy tale themes of high school romance. But, now as a woman, playing at love feels more like *Russian Roulette* than *Spin the Bottle*. So, instead of following every Tom, Dick, or Harry like an innocent lamb naively on its way to the slaughter, are you ready to lead like a lioness into your life? Instead of thrashing through a thousand Cracker Jacks boxes, gambling your hopes on finding the plastic ring, are you ready to go for the gold?

Instead of trusting that all you need to know about love you learned in high school, are you ready to launch your leap from preschool to Ph.D. in learning how to discern frog from prince? Instead of hoping George Clooney somehow spies your calm and beautiful face, and simply must swoop you out of a crowd of screaming groupies to live forever in his mansion by the sea, are you ready to make your own dazzling entrance as the leading lady of your life amidst the sea of spotlights and red carpet, casually glancing in the direction of those who would kill to take you to dinner? In other words, are you ready to shift your question from *Will he like me?* to **Is he WORTHY of Me?**

> **I do not wish women to have power over men,**
> **but over themselves.**
> Mary Wollstonecraft Shelley (1797 - 1851)

You hold within you the power that has held men in awe since the dawn of time. Trust that power to change what's not working in your search for love. Trust that power to change what's not working in your life. Trust that power to guide your journey to become *NaughtABimbeaux*.

Your Transition from *bimbo* to *NaughtABimbeaux* replaces:

- Panic with **POWER**
- Desperation with **DIGNITY**
- Terror with **TRUST**
- Wishes with **WISDOM**

Within these pages you will find guidance and support to empower your journey, such as information for your head, inspiration for your heart, invitation to your child within, and suggested questions for journaling each step you take into the life you are creating. Through the Mirror Magic exercise, you will affirm every day that you love yourself first, last and always.

At times, your journey may be reminiscent of *Mr. Toad's Wild Ride*. Other times you will single handedly confront all the terrorizing, fire breathing dragons commonly known as *your fears*. In other moments, you will embrace the radiance of your own worth. Expect laughter. Expect tears. Expect that with every step you take your journey is leading you to the place you long to be. Everything that happens from here on is in your hands.

> *You must have control of the authorship of your own destiny.*
> *The pen that writes your life story*
> *must be held in your own hand.*
> Irene Kassorla

JOURNEY JOURNALING:

Journaling your own story honors your past, present and future. If journaling is new to you, try starting slowly by jotting down a few words each day. Likely, it won't take long before you really get daring and start to write like a wild child! So, go for it! Write every hope, fear, and crazy idea. Write the vision that excites you. Write who you really are.

The questions below may give you some important answers. It's your choice to answer some or all. I promise you, the more questions you answer the more you clarify your TRUTH, and TRUTH is what your journey is all about.

What emotions came up as I read the definition for *bimbo*?

For *NaughtABimbeaux*?

Where in my body did I feel them?

Who came to mind as I felt them?

How does my pattern in relationships compare to Kathleen's?

How would my life change by taking care of myself first?

What is my level of commitment to this process?

What will I change to protect myself from another broken heart?

What will I change to know *Is he fraud or Is he forever?*

What fears am I willing to face to say, think, and feel what I have worked my whole life to avoid?

What do I want more than anything else?

What do I hope for more than anything else?

What do I dream of more than anything else?

MIRROR MAGIC: *I love you.*

RECOMMENDED READS:

The 16 Personality Types: Descriptions for Self-Discovery
by Linda V. Berens

Please Understand Me II: Temperament, Character, Intelligence
by David Keirsey.

*The Goddess in Every Woman: Powerful Archetypes in Women's
Lives* by Jean Shinoda Bolen

***To get through the hardest journey you need only to take one step
at a time, but you must keep on stepping.***
Chinese proverb

A word about Soul Mates: You read the chapter titles. You saw that
the last chapter describes your soul mate, so you know we will get to
him, eventually. But soul mates are like shoes. When you hold one half
of a pair of to-die-for shoes at Nordstroms Rack, you know immediately
when you find its mate because they're a **perfect match**. Recognizing
your soul mate works the same way. The only difference is that instead
of heel height, style, and color, you are matching two people who complement each other. Today all you hold in your hand is you, and just like
that pair of shoes, before you can recognize your mate you first need to
be very clear about **you**.

What is your life style, and your commitment to your health and
well-being? What are your personality traits, your hobbies, your habits?
What are your core values, and hopes and dreams for life and love?
What do you fear? What brings you joy?

It's said that opposites attract, but love for a lifetime only lasts when
the lovers are walking in the same direction.

Wherever you go, go with all your heart.
Confucius

On Becoming NaughtABimbeaux

2 What are You Pretending Naught to Know?

Excavating Your Truth

The Greek word for truth ~ Aletha ~ means 'not hidden.'
Catherine Kober

The unexamined life is not worth living.
Plato

What would happen if one woman
told the truth about her life?
The world would split open
Muriel Rekeyser

Our Terms:

PRETEND: To make believe; to cause or attempt to cause what is not so to seem so.

DENIAL: Disbelief in the existence or reality of something.

SELF-DENIAL: Reduction of anxiety by the unconscious exclusion from intolerable thoughts, feelings, or facts.

KNOW: To perceive or understand as fact or truth; to understand clearly and with certainty; to be aware of circumstance and all relevant data through observation, study, or experience.

TRUTH: The indisputable and verifiable fact or reality.

CAROL

Confused and hopeless after her second divorce, Carol found herself in San Francisco attending one of those infamous actualization seminars. She had invested significant money and time in her hope that *experts* could teach her the secret of finding a man. And, not just any man. Carol was very clear that this time she would find the man who would love her *till death do us part.*

The seminar was an intense experience ~ emotionally charged with more information and catharsis than one body could possibly absorb. And for all the strategic presentation, staged choreography and manipulated emotional wrenching, all that Carol took away was one simple phrase made up of seven words.

Hundreds of people would enter the ballroom of the grand hotel on that first evening, strangers bonded only by their shared fear of not being sure exactly what they had signed up for, or who would be traveling these four days alongside of them. As usual, Carol arrived early. She purposefully sat in a back row hoping to disappear into the crowd. She also hoped the event would begin so her anxiety would calm down. As she waited, she noticed a small banner taped to the wall behind the podium. The banner was so small she had to squint to read it. ***What are you pretending not to know?*** Thinking this was an interesting question, she promptly wrote it on the note pad she had brought along just in case someone said something worth remembering.

As the four days passed, Carol found it curious that each time everyone returned to the conference room after a break, that small banner had grown a bit larger. None of the speakers ever acknowledged the banner, or its provocative question that was obviously glaring from the wall behind them. Seemingly on its own and with no recognition, the banner just magically grew. By the final day, the banner filled the entire wall! … ***What are you pretending not to know?***

Driving home after that final day, Carol felt disappointed that her hope and investment of time and money to learn the secret of

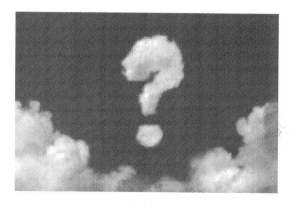

finding true love had not been answered. She felt stupid that all she really remembered was that silly question that now seemed to have an uncomfortable grip on her mind. Always one for a challenge, and weary of love's dead ends, Carol decided that if this question was all she remembered, maybe it would be important to take it seriously. Even though she didn't understand why it might be significant, she would answer it when it came to her mind. Whether it whispered in her ear or jolted her from her sleep, she vowed to answer it every time. To begin, she started with baby steps.

She asked her kids, *How was your day?* They predictably responded, *huh?* If she was lucky, they'd attempt to answer with their version of *I don't know*, as in, *I dunno.* So, Carol asked adults simple questions and, sure enough, often they answered, *I don't know.* She also noticed that this non-answer answer was rarely, if ever, questioned. Carol began to wonder if the human race had all agreed that *I don't know* was the one universal, excusable, default answer to any question that one might be asked.

Carol's intrigue grew. She questioned why she didn't just give an honest answer to an honest question if she did, indeed, know the answer. She questioned what purpose did denying even simple truth serve. She questioned how even her children would have already learned such strange behavior? Were we all resisting thinking? Or, as the question asked, were we pretending not to know what we knew? But, why would anyone do that? After some time, Carol also wondered why she had never thought about this before.

Before long she had established the habit of answering her simple everyday *What am I pretending not to know?* questions. She had to admit that this simple exercise ~ answering honestly of what she knew ~ had somehow shifted something inside of her, although she couldn't tell you exactly what. The more Carol truthfully answered her easy questions, the more curious she became about what other answers were lurking in the hidden places of her mind. She began to sense she might find her one most important answer there. Then a strange thing happened. Out of nowhere her questions began to take her back in time.

At first, most of them dealt with her first marriage ~ all the issues around her courtship, husband, marriage, divorce, and her children. True to her word, Carol answered honestly what she had been pretending not to know. After a few weeks questions came about high school boyfriends, girlfriends, grades, and sports. Again, though often appearing at inconvenient times, Carol opened up to listen for her answers, and always they would magically appear.

Then came the shift that changed everything. When her childhood memories brought up questions that wanted answers, she began to feel fear creeping in. So, Carol asked herself, *Why fear, why now? Is there something I'm **really** pretending not to know? Is fear trying to stop my questioning?* Again, wanting to be loved kept Carol resolute. The more fear she felt, the more she stayed with the process. She kept her journal in her purse at work and by her bed at night. She wrote everything that came to her mind until no thought or emotional response was censored. Finally came the day when, as if rewarding her honesty, the wall that had kept her deepest secrets hidden, and her life unfulfilled, came tumbling down. That was the day her mind finally brought forward the **real** question that would answer all the others. *What am I pretending not to know because Daddy stole my innocence when I was just a little girl?* At that point, flooded with emotion, Carol sought out a very wise, empathetic therapist recommended by one of her friends. Together, they safely invited the deepest and darkest of secrets to come into the light. Through that delicate process, and after all those years of questioning what was wrong with her, Carol had her answer. Nothing.

> ### *Only what is revealed can be healed.*
> Author Unknown

Today, Carol is an extraordinary woman. Her radical self-honesty birthed compassion for all the horror she had endured. Now the only time she *pretends* is when her granddaughters request such lovely things as a *Teddy Bear Tea Party* or a carriage ride to the Ball. But when Carol shares with them the wisdom of a wise and caring grandmother, the pretending ends.

As Carol eventually discovered, truthfully answering *What am I pretending not to know?* was her key to break free of her past and discover the woman she was born to be. Like Carol, when you honestly answer *What am I pretending not to know?* your truth will illuminate the path for all that lies ahead in your journey. **Your commitment to answer honestly is the key that will set you free.** Like Carol discovered, it won't be easy, but it will be worth all the risks you take to release the wonder of the woman you truly are.

The Child Learns to Cope by Doing What She Does Naturally.
She Pretends the Truth isn't Real.
She Pretends Not to Know.

Conscious parents know their child is dependent on their care and comfort. They know they live in the real world while children live in pretend lands of fairy tales and super heroes. They understand that their child's only reality is the one they give them, so sofas turn into forts, imaginary friends sit down for dinner, and magical stories are read over and over and over again.

Unfortunately, the real world is far from perfect. Very real adult dramas and traumas can intrude and overwhelm a parent's ability to nurture their child. Raised in fear, the child's birthright to be safe and nurtured can be lost in the chaos of adult concerns. So, rather than laughter and lullabies, a baby's brain absorbs confusion and panic. Imagine being dependent on big people for survival, yet powerless to understand or change your reality when they fail you. Imagine being unable to either flee or fight while living in a world beyond your ability to understand. Imagine being little and caught in such a no-win dilemma. When you are just too young to know why, fear replaces peace and doubt replaces security. To survive chaos, you learn to cope by doing what children do naturally. You pretend. You pretend reality isn't real. **You pretend not to know.**

> *We are born innocent. We are still innocent.*
> Sarah McLachlan

When one is young, it's impossible to understand why the people you depend on can't care for each other or you. Your child mind is incapable of disconnecting your reality from theirs, so your innate ability to pretend protects you, precious little Damsel in Distress, from the fear that swallows you up. Pretending is how you built the wall around your heart to keep it safe. But when childhood pretending evolves into adult denial, this is definitely not a good thing, for your current denial is no longer just a childhood quick-fix.

But wait! Denial Diva protests! *There is no wall! I'm just more comfortable pretending my past is past. So, let's just skip this chapter and get on with finding my prince. I mean, really... seven words to change my life? Besides, 'I don't know' has worked just fine for me so far.*

> *You never find yourself until you face your truth.*
> Pearl Bailey

Unless your mental capacities severely limit your self-awareness, you do know your own truth, especially the truth of how lonely you are. So when you continue to answer **I don't know** to love's important questions, your heart braces for what's coming ~ **the pain that keeps you dating men who bring you pain.** You know the routine. You tell yourself, *This time I won't be hurt. This time he will love me. This time the fairytale will come true.* And, let's be honest, we all know how those make-believe beliefs never seem to lead to *happily ever after.*

Remember those shoe mates at Nordstroms? Might that example have some relevance here? If you live in denial might you keep attracting men who live in denial, too? And, if that's your pattern, how is that working out for you? By the way, isn't changing that vicious cycle the reason you bought this book?

> *Inner pain is not evidence of defectiveness or inadequacy,*
> *but a signal that you are in need of comforting.*
> Tom Rusk M.D.

Finding Your Soul Mate Depends on Knowing Your Own Truth

Your journey, like Carol's, begins with answering, *What am I pretending not to know?* whenever, wherever it appears. Trust me, in the beginning you may feel stupid, maybe even irritated as you stop your life to answer, because breaking your everyday routine can feel inconvenient, even uncomfortable. Of course, questions like *What do I want for dinner? Why am I uncomfortable being here?* or *How do I want to spend this weekend?* do seem meaningless in the big scheme of things. Even so, answer anyway because every time you answer, you train your brain to keep you honest.

A word of warning: Chances are good, like Carol, that this pesky 7 word question will wake you in the night or when you're rushing to an appointment. Admittedly, that can be annoying. Yet, as crazy as it may sound, whenever *What am I pretending not to know?* pops into your head, stop and be still as your mind and heart search for the answer. If doing that is truly impossible in the situation, at least take one minute to write down the details of the circumstances you were in when the question came, then as soon as you can, find a quiet place and wait for the answer. If you're open, I promise you it will come. It's already there.

Since we're talking about honesty, let's be honest here. If you have lived a life of impulsive choices, desperation, denial, anxiety and avoidance, stopping your life while you coax your real truth out of hiding ~ every single scary, overwhelming, tragic, bizarre, boring bit of it ~ will likely feel awful. So, why is answering in the moment so crucial? Because neither the question nor your answer will wait while you find a convenient time…as that's been your problem all along. The love you want can't breathe in denial, only in truth. Being self-aware is Step #1 to becoming *NaughtABimbeaux*.

Fear = Self-denial = **Self-sabotage**
Peace = Self-awareness = **Truth**

Would living free from fear be worth your promise that whenever your mind, heart and soul want to answer *I don't know*, you will step out of the craziness of your life until your nervous twitching, fast forwarding Denial Diva mentality accepts that becoming honest can be scary, yet you will face your fear anyway? Are you willing to wait for your truth to come forward? Are you willing to be still and answer with the truth of who you truly are?

It is good to have an end to the journey,
but it is the journey that matters in the end.
Ursula K. Le Guin

JOURNEY JOURNALING:

What is one small question that I am pretending not to know the answer?

What could be my reason(s) for avoiding a truthful answer?

What am I willing to do to change this pattern? Why?

What will I do whenever THE question appears?

What did I pretend not to know growing up in my home?

What three feelings am I experiencing now?

How do these feelings affect my commitment to becoming NaughtABimbeaux?

What do I fear most about entering this journey?

MIRROR MAGIC: *I love you.*

RECOMMENDED READS:

Feel the Fear and Do It Anyway by Susan Jeffers, Ph.D.

Getting Real: Ten Truth Skills You Need to Live by Susan Campbell, Ph.D.

To encourage you…

As you shine light on all you have hidden, you will gather up all the heartbreak endured by the little girl who once was, and is still you. Your journey began with her first steps. If you have a childhood picture, look into her face and see what her eyes are telling you. Promise to protect and nurture her as you, the woman, learn to be wise. Talk to her as you lead her hand in hand through this journey. You are all she has, and she has hoped for you since you left her behind so many years ago.

> *Sometime in your life you will go on a journey.*
> *It will be the longest journey you have ever taken.*
> *It is the journey to find yourself.*
> Katherine Sharp

Note:

It is not often that to begin a journey one steps backwards. But, in Chapter 3 you will still keep stepping backward in time. Not until Chapter 4 will you move forward, and maybe decide you don't ever need to look back, again.

You do have a wild ride ahead of you between here and Chapter 20. If you're absolutely serious about becoming *NaughtABimbeaux* then how you respect the truth of this chapter will be fundamental to the success of your journey. Take your time. I did not write this book as a *quick read*. I wrote it to support your journey ~ **for as long as it takes** ~ for you to understand how valuable, how worthy, how wonderful, and how deserving you are of the love you want. For most of us, believing all of that takes time. So, please, take time. Excavate your truth. Then, trust it as if your dreams depended on it. The rest of the book will wait for you, I promise.

Cautionary Note:

On Becoming NaughtABimbeaux is not a replacement for psychotherapy. One in three of America's daughters experience deep sanctuary betrayal, most often by biological or stepfathers, uncles, brothers, baby-sitters, neighbors, clergy, teachers, coaches or family friends. At any time on your journey if you experience any sense of emotional intensity, if you find yourself on the verge of break down rather than break through, please stop reading and seek professional support with a therapist you trust who specializes in such issues. Often times, this road is a long and rocky one for survivors, but it is one that is necessary to reclaim your life. Wait until you feel stronger to take the following steps offered here, or to take them in smaller steps with a compassionate therapist trained in betrayal issues. Healing childhood wounding is not an easy process. In the end, though, you will know the journey to healing has been worth every brave step you took.

3 *Once Upon a Lifetime:*
Lasting Impressions of Your
1st Prince Charming

Old as she was, she still missed her daddy sometimes.
Gloria Naylor

It doesn't matter who my father was. It matters who
I remember he was.
Anne Sexton

Our Terms:

FATHER: Man who gives paternal care to others; protector, provider; to take responsibility for; a leading man.

SANCTUARY: A place providing safety and refuge; safe harbor in a storm; a place where the core feelings of the heart are nurtured.

BETRAYAL: The act of deceiving, seducing, leading astray; abandon.

DADDY ~ Never a Neutral Word

Once upon a long time ago, the mythological gods of Greece discovered that daddies hold the power to delight or destroy their daughters. Once upon our modern time, the gods of neuro-science scratch their heads wondering just how the ancient Greeks figured that out. How is it that when a baby girl enters center stage into the opening act of *This is My Life*, her baby brain already knows her daddy has won the supporting role as her first Prince Charming, and, upon her grand entrance, will court her like a Princess at the Ball?

When modern science finally cues in on that answer, it will also likely explain why you followed him everywhere, like a toddling Cinderella shadowing her Prince, so eager to begin their dance.

Back when I was a child, before life removed all the innocence, my father would lift me high and dance with my mother and me, and then spin me around 'til I fell asleep. Then up the stairs he would carry me, and I knew for sure I was loved. If I could get another chance, another walk, another dance with him, I'd play a song that would never, ever end. How I'd love, love, love to dance with my father, again.
Luther Vandross

Sometimes a daddy shows up in his little girl's life like a seasoned actor. Not only has he read the script, he has memorized his lines, researched his role, and set his sights on winning an Oscar. As his daughter's 1st Prince Charming, teaching her to dance the dance of life is the greatest gift of his life!

When he raised you up in his arms, you trusted him with the music of your soul. As he raised you up in your life, you learned how wonderful and freeing real love feels like.

But, in time you would grow suspect. Had he always known that your shared dance was preparing you for every dance to follow? Had he always known you two were simply rehearsing for the day you would dance in white with your Prince for life?

Tender, nurturing fathers have proven quite effective when one hopes to launch a confident, capable and centered daughter to dance her own way out into her world. If yours was one of those daddies, the stories in this chapter will read like pure fiction for these stories represent the millions of women, who in millions of ways, have been betrayed by the man they were born to trust more than any other.

LIZ

Liz was the only woman on a team of investment bankers specializing in corporate takeovers of vulnerable companies. She was on her way up and hardly noticed people on their way down. The corporate world promotes people like Liz. Her friends nicknamed her Dynamo, and occasionally risked asking, *Liz, do you ever relax?* Her typical answer would be, *Sure. Last night after dinner I read the SEC's newest ruling on insider trading. I was totally relaxed.*

Liz grew up with a dinner ritual where her father reminded her of his struggle to get to the top, and without a son it was up to her to ensure his legacy. *Make me proud, Lizzy*, he'd say dryly, as she struggled to smile and not choke on her food. She also struggled to compete in three honors classes, star in the drama club, and maintain her ranking for the tennis A team. In the middle of her junior year, her psychiatrist prescribed medication for anxiety.

Liz knew that pleasing *Dear Daddy* hinged on a high school transcript that would impress the right college. So, it was full-force panic that drove her to be the perfect student. She always sat in the front row, raised her hand to answer first, and stayed up past midnight to write the perfect paper that somehow never quite met that mark. Her B+ average didn't ever seem to concern anyone ~ anyone except him, and except her.

Muting his sports channel, he would glance up as she handed him her less than 4.0 report card, her already anxious stomach churning. As his glance turned to ice, her tense tummy turned to stone. Typically, she waited for him to notice she'd brought up her English grade, or earned an A in biology, and every teacher commended her effort. Instead, he'd ceremoniously sign the card, put it back in her hand, look her in the eye and sigh, *For goodness sakes, Lizzy, next time make me proud.*

Daddy never cared that the only course his daughter consistently failed was Romance 101. As he saw it, his role as Daddy was to tell Liz when to jump and how high. If she did jump at the right time and high enough, he'd hand her a morsel of affection, much in the same way you give a dog a few scraps from the table.

But even his pressure couldn't overrule a normal adolescent female's hormones that were raging inside her body. After all, teenage girls just wouldn't be teenage girls without a little love in their lives. With only an occasional hug from her father, Liz had a huge hole in her heart and an adolescent mind to figure out how to fill it.

She came up with what she thought was the perfect solution. Given that her primary male role model valued perfection, she transformed into the teenage equivalent of a Stepford Wife. She was primed to be perfect at using compliance as seduction. Predictably, it always ended with her latest *flame of the month* bored and looking for someone new. Then, with each break-up, Liz would break down, relying on her prescriptions to dry her tears and get her back on daddy's treadmill.

The day after her 18th birthday, she watched her parents drive away as she was left standing alone in front of her college dorm. The next morning, scrambling past hundreds of fellow freshmen, Liz was racing to get into classes that would someday help her climb the corporate ladder. Her face radiated confidence; her tummy shook like jello as that familiar voice whispered in her ear, the voice that had always questioned her value, her intelligence, her looks, and especially her sanity to think she could ever compete.

Fear-driven, but determined, six years later with her MBA in hand, Liz launched into a promising career, and a considerably less promising marriage. Now that she had traded her dignity for a diamond, Liz felt secure enough with her new husband to take off her Stepford mask and be herself ~ the self that never ever admitted defeat. He, on the other hand, had rather warmed to the idea of a wife who lived by the motto… *Whatever you want, Sweetheart.* Liz' new-found confidence not only surprised him, it threatened his ego and their imbalance-of-power arrangement. The true ego-driven Liz was not the wife he had bargained for. Before she could defrost the top tier of her wedding cake in celebration of their first anniversary, the marriage that had never really begun was over.

Running from her question, *What is wrong with me?* Liz became even more ruthless at the corporate game. Well, at least until the next attractive GQ man happened to cross her path. In the wink of his eye, Corporate Liz would crumble like crackers into the most compliant woman she could fake herself to be. Too bad Romance 202 wasn't offered as a post-graduate course.

Each relationship launched with her high hopes, lots of lust, and Liz' aim to compromise her power to hang on to love. But, like always, such illusion degenerated into vicious bickering between two powerful, but childish egos fighting for control.

Finally, after an especially humiliating break-up with a man who Liz knew all along was a step-down from what she deserved, she faced the facts. She had to change or she'd be alone forever. So, she booked her first appointment with the best therapist in town. In her initial session Liz explained that men didn't understand her, and that they were often threatened by her corporate position of power. The therapist nodded knowingly. She then asked Liz to just look inside herself and tell her what she saw. When Liz was able to answer a few moments later, *All I see is black, like there's nothing there,* the therapist recognized a woman who had lost herself, probably for a very long time.

In the following session, Liz confessed that she felt so tired of feeling empty every time she watched another man walk out her door, especially after she had vowed to do her best to hold onto him. Then, in a moment of truth, she heard her own voice say, *My dilemma is essentially being the CEO at work and the janitor in my relationships.* Liz and her therapist both looked stunned! What Liz had just realized was that this just didn't make any sense, and Liz's life had to make sense. Over the weeks, behind the safety of those closed doors, Liz journeyed back into childhood memories. She was surprised by how much everything that happened years ago felt so present, as if her little girl's pain was still so fresh. Her therapist encouraged her to journal daily for the next four weeks. She was to let her thoughts guide what each day's journaling would be about. On the tenth day, it was as if Liz's pen took over. She started writing with one intention ~ to finally bring out into the open what she'd never had the nerve to see or say before.

And here is what her heart guided her pen to write: *You looked, but you didn't see. You heard, but you didn't listen. I was just a little girl. I needed you to be my protector, my cheerleader, my Superman. I know you didn't set out to hurt your daughter, but Daddy, you did. You would only love me if I was perfect. But I couldn't be perfect ~ nobody can be perfect. But because that was what you taught me, I've lost any hope that someone will love me for who I am.*

Liz's desperation for a man to notice her did not happen by accident. She had lived a life groveling to get her daddy's attention. She grew up repressed and empty from her father's narcissism, and then transferred her yearning to choose men as emotionally unavailable and toxic as he had been. This emotional hunger led her into an adult paradox of living as a human *door mat* while seeking emotionally detached, perfection-istic men who walked all over her. Even though she was a competent woman, she remained caught in a vicious cycle of relentlessly trying not to be the woman her father told her she would become. Before Liz finally took the courageous step to investigate this deepest of personal issues ~ the father-daughter relationship ~ she had demeaned herself to so many men that she'd long ago lost count.

> **Sometimes your only available transportation**
> **is a leap of faith.**
> Margaret Shepard

All children are born egocentric. So when a father is demanding, demeaning, destructive or distant, his daughter believes she deserves it. Tragically, when a father breaks his little girl's trust, she believes it's because she's not worthy of it. If your daddy's own dysfunction trumped your childhood needs to be safe and nurtured, you learned to live desperate to just keep his attention. When you cried, *Watch me, Daddy!* was he there? When you marched up on stage with your second-grade class, was he in the audience cheering you on? Did he insist on a perfect performance of his little princess, and if you weren't just so, did he let you know that you had failed him?

Without you ever being aware, everything you needed to know about being a woman depended on how well your *1st Love* loved you. How he treated you became your model for how you expect all men to treat you as a woman. If he didn't cherish you for who you were, it's no surprise you have difficulty now taking yourself seriously in a romantic relationship, for the past issues between you and your father have become today's issues between you and your intimate partner.

SARAH

Sarah stood in front of her mirror and stared at the stranger staring back. *Who **are** you?* She watched her question escape her mouth, but heard no answer coming back.

Over the years, Sarah's friends had given up asking about her family, for on that subject she was strangely silent. And, since she was always willing to listen while others talked about theirs, no one seemed to mind. The rare comments she did make hinted that her home had never been a place where a little girl could cuddle up in front of the TV with her daddy, laughing at Bert and Ernie trying to talk Oscar the Grouch out of his garbage can. Oh, if only Sarah's father had been just a harmless green grouch rather than Oscar's evil twin.

It was always difficult to predict what would light his short fuse at the end of a long day. He would come through the front door after a long shift of policing the city streets, lay his gun, still in its holster, on the dresser and walk into the kitchen. If they heard that certain sound in his voice and saw his eyes turn evil, each one could feel the air being sucked out of the room for they knew this would be one of those nights. Maybe the Captain had criticized his paperwork on an arrest, or a bike had innocently blocked the driveway. Maybe dinner was too hot, or his beer not cold enough. But, when the tension was this tight, Sarah's mother stopped whatever she was doing and started pleading and pushing her children out of the room. Sarah knew to run, but her brothers would stay, trying to protect her and their mother even though they were no match for their father. In the aftermath, he had thrown his empty bottle of booze into the wall, Sarah's mother was bruised, her brothers were banished from the house, and Sarah was hiding in her closet, curled up in a ball and shaking with terror. The damage was indescribable so nobody did.

Little Sarah thought she could soothe her daddy with kindness. For days after of one those *episodes* she would tiptoe around him to bring him his paper, or bake his favorite cookies, or rub his neck while she sang a little song he once told her he liked. She would have done anything to not let it happen again, to have peace in her home. But, of course, despite her sweetness and hope, it always did happen again. This is how Sarah remembered, but never spoke of her childhood.

A few years later, high school parties became her excuse to escape, especially when her dad wasn't on patrol. She worried about leaving her mom alone with him, but she liked it when boys flirted with her, especially the jocks. In her senior year she started going out with Jason, a football player who, at first, treated her like a queen. He carried her books, sneaked her off campus at lunch, and helped her with math. Her heart was so hungry for affection she hardly noticed that at weekend parties, once he was drunk, he'd boast that she belonged to him, and then threaten any guy who looked at her. Sarah loved when he talked that way. She felt safe and protected, until the night he raped her.

They'd been going steady for almost six months when Jason caught her talking with a guy from the track team at a friend's party. In front of everyone, he yanked her off the couch, yelling obscenities and pushing her to the floor while he went after his rival. At the same time, Sarah felt her body freeze. In her mind she was racing for her closet. An hour later, as she pleaded, *No, Jason, NO!* he pushed himself into her as they lay straddled across the front seats of his car. When it was over, Jason calmed down and drove her home. It was while they were standing under the porch light that he saw the bruises on her arms. *Sarah, I'm so sorry. I swear I'll never hurt you, again. It just really pissed me off to see you with another guy.* Sarah, with all sincerity, told him, *It's not that bad, baby. I'll wear long sleeves for a few days, and nobody will notice.* But nobody noticing only lasted until her brothers heard about what Jason had done to their little sister. They threatened him that if he ever touched their sister again they'd kill him. From that night on, Sarah suffered alone with the inner struggle between the horror of rape, the titillation of the sex, and the paralyzing fear if her father ever found out.

Eventually, all three siblings escaped to college and careers far from their hometown. Sarah moved two states away with a friend she'd known since kindergarten, and started classes at a community college. She dated once in a while, but the slightest sign of *macho* would make her break it off. Even if the guy seemed nice, if he raised his voice at all, Sarah knew men didn't stop until someone got hurt.

She called home often, and could always hear in her mother's voice when she'd had a bad night. Sarah's guilt for deserting her mother kept her awake at night, but she could not bring herself to go home. She made up flimsy excuses, knowing her mom didn't believe her. Neither would her mom accept her offer of a ticket to come for a visit.

All that changed on the night her mother phoned at 2 AM. With a voice Sarah hardly recognized, she heard her coldly say, *Daddy was shot trying to stop a robbery. He died on the way to the hospital.* Sarah's first thought was not shock, but rather, *Strange, I always thought he was invincible.*

Two days later, she was meeting her brothers at their hometown airport. There was only silence as they drove together in the rental car to the house. When they saw their mother standing alone, looking lost and pitiful in that familiar driveway, none of them could hold back tears as they rushed to hold her. Within the hour, one lone limousine arrived to drive them to the funeral. Only their mother knew who would escort them afterwards to the cemetery. Since he'd been killed in the line of duty, not only did they have a police escort, but hundreds of police stood in dress uniform to honor their fallen comrade at the gravesite. Eulogies by the precinct Captain and their parish priest spoke in glowing platitudes of his valor and commitment to the safety of their city's citizens. After the final prayer, one lone bugler stood on a nearby hill and played *Amazing Grace*. At the funeral just one hour before, his widow and children had looked into the coffin. The sight of his stiff, cold body assured them that he was indeed dead. The monster was really dead. Also dead was their dream that this husband and father would ever really love them. Not one of them shed a tear as the coffin dropped into the earth.

One week later, Sarah caught a morning flight home, where her childhood friend picked her up and drove her straight to the best spa in town. She'd known Sarah all her life. She knew these past few days had been rough for her friend.

Still stressed from the events of the past week, not to mention her childhood, thirty minutes later Sarah was lying on a massage table feeling gentle fingers press deep into her tissues. Such gentle touch felt so strange, so unexpected that her body shivered. The massage therapist urged her, *Go with it. Make any sounds or movements you feel. Just trust your body to release its suffering.* Such inviting permission opened Sarah to uncontrollable sobbing. Her body shook on the table and it scared her. She wasn't comfortable with feeling vulnerable. She was unfamiliar with the compassion of a stranger. Later, as she sat in the steam room, her body still trembled and the tears still fell. Before she left the spa, she had scheduled a massage for the following week.

The shift was gradual. As often occurs in grief, Sarah's subconscious mind took about four to six weeks to begin absorbing the factual evidence that her father had truly died. She still expected her mom to whisper when she phoned home, or if he answered, to hear for the millionth time how worthless she was for leaving. Nightmares appeared as her subconscious mind feared he'd risen from the dead, then come to her enraged, in the middle of the night, to watch her sleep as his eyes flashed the color of cold steel. The horror would jolt her awake as she found her pillow wet with tears. In the morning, she reminded herself of the sweet peace she had felt when she stood at the grave site, knowing that he could not hear the bugle playing in his honor.

The good father does not have to be perfect.
Rather, he has to be good enough to help his daughter to become a
woman who is reasonably self-confident, self-sufficient, and free of
crippling self-doubt, and to feel at ease in the company of men.
Victoria Secunda

As Sarah healed, she began flying home to visit her mom. She couldn't hide her smile when she saw the woman who had birthed her now dressed in flattering clothes and playing a once-forbidden jazz CD, as she explained, for *atmosphere.* She had enrolled in an art class where she was meeting new friends, especially an intriguing widower who always set up his easel next to hers.

Over the next several visits, Sarah helped hang her beautiful watercolors on the walls of the home that had once held such terror. They planted a garden out in the back and shared long walks through the woods on the edge of town. Then, one morning as they sat at that same table in that once haunted kitchen, Sarah put her tea cup in its saucer and risked the question, *Why, Mom?* Sarah's mother looked into her daughter's eyes and for the first time told her the truth. *He was a cop. He could have tracked us down. He told me he would, and not if, but when he found us, that would be the end.*

Sarah's childhood model for an intimate relationship consisted of terror and chaos. For both women in this family, their fear kept them stuck, unable to realize other options, other resources, other ways of taking care of themselves. Such *learned helplessness* is typical in fear-based families where women and children are denied any sense of respect or equity. Sarah's mother chose to live within the confines of her home, basically laying down her life for her children. Sarah and her brothers escaped that family home, but her brothers were habitually attracted like moths to the flame into power and control relationships. Only Sarah chose to break free from her family's cycle of violence, inviting into her life only friends and lovers who shared her commitment to living a conscious and peaceful life.

As was true of Sarah's story, living as though nothing horrible happened is often the only means of handling overwhelming emotions that come with growing up in terror. Sarah coped by running away from her father's rage, first to her closet, then to illicit sex, and then moving two states away and closing her heart. She lived as so many others do, limping forward into the rest of her life. When the source of violence is removed, either through desertion, divorce, incarceration or death, some victims may feel adequately released to come out from hiding and face the truth of their victimization and move through their pattern of denial into living an authentic life. Many others require support and guidance from their families, friends, or a therapist trained and sensitive to the deep, ego-altering effects of family violence.

Wounds of childhood enter and remain in the body at the cellular level, so releasing the physical effects through body work can be critical for healing. For Sarah, the vulnerability of massage could have re-sparked her childhood helplessness. But, over time the gentleness and permission of the therapist allowed her to release her fear and experience the comfort of being nurtured. Once her body had released much of the tension, her mind was able to invite that frightened little girl to come out into the light.

Love's the greatest healer to be found.
Willie Nelson

LYNN

When Lynn's father wasn't out of town on business, he violated her almost daily, from the age of three until she left home after high school. When her daddy was away, her stepbrother happily took over for him. By the time she entered fifth grade, the fact that she was a sexualized child was obvious as her appearance and actions spoke volumes. Her skirts were short, her smile pouty. She flirted with every male teacher and draped herself across boys' desks like a velvet curtain. Teacher concerns about her promiscuous behavior dominated parent conferences, with her father and mother listening attentively, followed by their hollow promises to seek counseling for their wayward daughter.

As sexual violation was all she'd known, Lynn grew into a woman expecting and accepting abuse from men. To medicate away the deep, deep pain of her fractured life, she became addicted to alcohol, drugs, and sex without limits. But whether in a stupor or sober, Lynn's heart could not break free of what her father had done to destroy the innocence of his very own little girl. Finally, when a concerned cousin took the risk to invite Lynn to a 12 step program, she accepted. At her first meeting, the speaker shared a surprisingly similar story to Lynn's. Listening to his words, she felt soothed, even hopeful. After the meeting, when he encouraged her to return the next day for another meeting, Lynn said *Yes*. Deep within her soul she intuitively knew that without help her life would continue to spiral downward.

Lynn's identity as a sexual object took hold early. With a father who trampled her innate need to be protected and valued, the attention she longed for was metered out only when she pleased him sexually, or at least did not spoil their rendezvous with too many tears. When being violated by her stepbrother, she let her tears flow freely.

For Lynn, any normal adult sense of self-worth and dignity was lost in having been dehumanized as a child. She was a normal woman wanting to be loved, but her childhood tapes played in her head the warped messages of how she should *earn* it. So, she wore grown up versions of her earlier precocious outfits, then mistook men's initial flattery for authentic interest. With the support of her 12-Step sponsor, she determined to become healthy in her body and her mind. Attending those meetings proved to be her first legitimate steps to break her generational cycle of family betrayal.

As a little girl, your father's words and actions held more power than any others because how he valued you as a child became how you value yourself as a woman. Even though long ago tucked away in your subconscious, if his messages harmed you, they quietly and insidiously migrate into your life now as the primary reason you sabotage your real hopes and dreams to be loved. Unaware, you act them out every day. When you are able to open your eyes and admit how deeply he hurt you, then it will become easier to recognize what nurtures you now.

> ***If you keep doing what you've always done,***
> ***you'll keep getting what you've always got.***
> Author Unknown

ANNIE

Annie was her father's favorite daughter. He often bragged that the night before her birth he knew she would be a girl and that she would be special. And, so she was.

Even though Daddy had declared Annie *perfect*, her sisters were held to a much higher standard. Neither the younger nor older were thrilled with this arrangement, so not surprisingly they plotted between them to make Annie's life hell. Annie's mother knew to not question anything her husband did, so if she felt any pangs of jealousy, she kept them to herself.

But nothing anyone said or did changed the fact that Annie was the apple of her Daddy's eye. He bought her princess dresses and Barbie dolls, her own pony, tennis lessons, and anything else her little heart desired. Annie chose the color of his new cars, and picked out his ties for work. He helped her with homework, let her win at Checkers, and was the last one, and often the only one, he kissed goodnight. On one of those nights after lights were out, Annie's older sister crept into her room, shined a flashlight in her face and whispered, *How's it feel to be Daddy's little girlfriend, sister dear?*

Not too many years later, Annie and her body were ready, eager and willing to replace Daddy with boys! It was no surprise when Annie's full-blown adolescence set him and his princess on a collision course that would eventually become so bitter neither ever recovered. She wanted to wear makeup. Daddy said *No!* So, she put it on when she got to school and wiped it off on her way home. When one Friday night he learned she was at her best friend's house for her first ever girl/boy party, he drove across town and dragged her home. Annie was mortified. Daddy was resolute. The battle lines were drawn.

Daddy forbid her to go to dances, so every Friday night Annie told him she was going bowling as she bolted out the front door knowing full well those weren't bowling shoes in her bag. (God help her if the day ever came he wanted to watch her try for a 300!)

Annie had worried since her freshman year about her Senior Prom, knowing how restrictive her father was about her dating. When his schedule had him out of town for a business conference on Prom weekend, she thought that problem was solved. Imagine her terror when he flew home one day early, the very day of the Prom. When Annie's date arrived at their door, Daddy towered above the poor unsuspecting boy as he told him his daughter wasn't available. Annie stood just out of sight, seething in her designer gown. As her date drove away in the limousine, she ran screaming to her room, slammed the door, and was nowhere to be found the next morning. Her parents reported her missing, and by Sunday afternoon, their little *wild child* had been found at her best friend's home.

Annie's father finally admitted he had been a bit too harsh over the years, but it was too late. It was he who had created a princess, and then treated her as a prisoner in her own castle. When she rebelled, he withdrew his affection at the most critical time that she needed him. His attempt at smoothing out the humiliation he caused his daughter was now intrusive and oppressive. If only he could have recognized that his rigidity to keep her as his daddy-dependent little girl wouldn't, couldn't, and shouldn't last because it was time for Annie to evolve from his little princess into a young woman.

With his excessive restrictions, their relationship became so estranged that even though the confidence he had instilled in her would eventually open doors of opportunity, her unrealistic reality cursed her with a sense of entitlement that turned men off as fast as they turned her on. Her dilemma was that she had no intention of staying her father's little princess, and he couldn't see past his fantasy to realize that Annie's breaking free was normal and healthy. Years later, though estranged, Annie was still obsessed with winning the control war with her father. This compulsion led to a *devil-may-care* life style that set her up for a breakdown before her 30th birthday. Once she was in adult relation-ships, she had to learn the hard way that intimacy is not the result of being more special than your partner. As with so many women with daddy issues, going through therapy was when Annie's reality hit a brick wall. There came the session when she realized that her father had used her as his *virgin mistress* to avoid any real intimacy with his wife. In reality, believing she was his princess, she had actually been his substitute lover. It would be years before Annie spoke to her father again. He had suffered a heart attack and Annie, wanting to resolve their story with a peaceful ending, went home to say *I forgive you, Daddy.*

> ### *You don't change your destiny by turning the faces*
> ### *of family portraits to the wall.*
> Jawaharlal Nehru

Annie and her sisters were all victims of their father's unbalanced attention, and their mother's passivity that allowed it to happen. There was never any overt abuse towards his daughters, just blindness to his own masculine insecurity that sadly, tragically impacted each of them in different ways. With Annie, he did everything right as far as being involved. He encouraged her, supported her education, listened to her little girl woes, and even took her to work with him. He did everything right, but for the wrong reasons. Annie's sisters had issues of a different kind. The early influence of their insecure father rippled out into their lives for years to come. Her older sister was obsessed with control; her younger sister never graduated from high school. Both were bitter, but then short-changed children often are.

PATRICIA

Before she chose her seat at the bar, Patricia always made sure there was an empty one next to hers. She would order the first of her evening's several gin and tonics, and then wait for the first handsome stranger in a three-piece suit to join her. She never waited long. Once he bought her next G & T, he'd either invite her back to his hotel room, or if she didn't play his game, he'd leave her to buy her own next drink.

Years before she acquired a taste for alcohol, little Patsy felt her body die for the first time. It was a sunny day as Mommy backed out of the driveway. Daddy took Patti's little hand and led her up the stairs to her parents' bed. She was eight years old.

The first time, he merely fondled her. Maybe he couldn't take himself further because, after all, she was his little girl. But, before summer's end, he had stolen her *virginity*. In 7th grade science she learned what that word meant. It would take a few more years before she understood what he had ripped from her heart and soul.

By the time she was a high school freshman, Daddy had already replaced her with her younger sister, and Patricia had replaced him with older men. Other than no longer sharing blood ties with her sex partners, nothing really changed except for her growing feeling of worthlessness blending with a complementary list of psychological disorders.

In spite of her lifestyle, Patricia had a keen intelligence. On her 23rd birthday, she graduated from college with a degree in Journalism. The demands of an education had allowed her mind several years to escape the emptiness, but once she was working an eight-hour shift at a local newspaper, the remaining sixteen hours opened up more time to think, to remember. Predictably, her old need to disconnect from the world around her, most of all from herself, returned to haunt her day and night.

Several years later, when drinking and late nights of illicit sex seriously interfered with her job performance, friends urged her into therapy. Thankfully, she was low enough to listen. She wasn't exactly sure what to expect, but she knew she couldn't escape from all the pain that left her feeling like the *walking dead*. She couldn't go on with the charade that was her life.

She told her therapist, *I have tried to be respectful of my father, but my childhood leaks into my relationships. It seems men sense they can control me. I felt that my father hated me, so I hated myself. I guess I still do. I remember trying to be a happy child, and that I kept hoping that something good was waiting for me, but it never was.*

At the urging of her therapist, Patricia attended a weekend self-help seminar for women. During the last session the therapist asked the forty participants to form a circle, and then respond to a significant question: *If any of you were molested as children, if you are willing, please step inside the circle.* At the end of three very long minutes, only eleven women remained on the outside. The twenty-nine souls standing inside the circle included teachers, bankers, executives, physicians, law enforcement, and mental health professionals. One of the first to step forward into the circle was Patricia.

> **Until you make the unconscious conscious, it will direct your life and you will call it fate.**
> Carl Jung

Innocence is the absence of fear. When innocence is stolen, a happy childhood becomes a heinous nightmare. The most common perpetrators for a little girl are her father, stepfather, brother, uncle, or mother's boyfriend(s). During such egregious violation, not only is her physical body invaded, but her fragile emerging ego holds the space for all that she is to become. In those moments that her pure little self is being shattered, his sexual invasion sows the seeds that will damage, sometimes destroy, her core *femaleness* as she matures.

For Patricia, therapy became the path to safely examine her father's toxicity. What she hadn't planned on was seeing that behind his destruction was her mother's silence that allowed the rape of her daughters in her own home, while she pretended she heard, saw, knew and felt nothing. Could anyone doubt that not only did Patricia have issues with men, but her mother's betrayal left her unable to trust anyone, male or female?

The fundamental ingredient in any woman's life is her relationship with her father. Their relationship will affect her relationships with all other men in her life. There's not a single relationship that isn't indelibly stamped - for good or for ill — by the man known as Daddy. Study after study show that fathers set up their daughters for success, whether or not they live in the same house as their daughters.
Dr. Keven Leman   *What a Difference a Daddy Makes: The Indelible Imprint a Dad Leaves on his Daughter's Life.*

These stories have focused on several father-daughter dynamics. One theme not addressed was if a father wasn't there, either physically or emotionally lost somewhere in his addiction to women, alcohol, drugs, sports, TV, money or power. This arrangement can appear less traumatizing than the overt violence of our stories, but nothing could be less true. Abandonment is abuse, and abuse in any form leaves a daughter with a suffocating sense of rejection, of not being adorable enough to win the one man she longed to have love her.

It is Human to Choose what is Familiar
Even if it is Spelled *Dysfunction*

As each of these individual stories reveal, it is not a twist of fate when a father's violation of his daughter leads to a woman's later desperation for a man, any man. No, all little girls are vulnerable to become who our daddies tell us we are.

Relationships are like a dance. It's as much about your patience, kindness, confidence, and sense of rhythm as it is your choice of partner.
Author Unknown

Dancing with the Stars is one the most successful TV shows ever produced. Millions tune in every week to watch a celebrity amateur and a professional create magic between them and us. The duos that win our votes week after week ooze confidence and chemistry with moves that take our breath away.

Other than the glamour and glitz, could the overwhelming popularity of DWTS be that those beautiful dancers reflect the romance we seek in real life? After all, wouldn't you want to dance with that same daring confidence with a partner who respects and adores you?

The one unbreakable rule of couples dancing is that the partners must move interdependently as a unit.
Author Unknown

They may make it look easy, but behind the scenes what we viewers don't see is what the celebrity dancers quickly learn ~ dancing to win starts with learning simple, yet unfamiliar steps. To get to the big stage, the celebrities spend hours on their own, surrounded by mirrors analyzing every step and misstep. Their instructors call them out, over and over again. Falling down happens. Hopeless frustration happens. Behind the closed doors of the rehearsal rooms, these normally confident Stars question their sanity and break down in tears. Then they question their fears. Then, because they want to win, they face those fears and keep dancing.

You have got to discover you, what you do, and trust it.
Barbra Streisand

If your daddy issues are still sabotaging your dance of love, learning how to take the lead in your own dance is how you release his *shadow* from your adult relationships. Of course, releasing his shadow from your dance may be one of the hardest things you will ever do, but learning to dance free from fear is the first step to learn how to dance free with your true partner. And, just as the celebrities, expect *falling down* to happen. Expect frustration to happen. Expect fear to happen. Be patient with yourself as you take baby steps to dance into your own life. After all, one does not leap from beginning ballet to the Bolshoi. Unlike with your father, no one can step on your toes or tell you that you are doing it wrong. With time and your courage, you will be ready to invite the one you can trust into your arms to share your life's dance. So, your question is: *Is the prize of your prince worth facing your fears?*

Do you remember in the Wizard of Oz when Toto's little body shook as he mustered up enough puppy courage to pull back those curtains? Remember, it was his courage that revealed that the Great and Powerful Oz was nothing more than a little man pulling levers that controlled flashing lights through smoke and mirrors? As soon as Toto's action revealed the truth, the scam was over. The Great and Powerful Oz was just a harmless coward cowering in front of Toto, a harmless but courageous little dog. It was Toto's feeling his fear and doing it anyway that had us all cheering!

> ***The moment in between who you once were, and who you are now becoming, is where the dance of life really takes place.***
> Barbara De Angelis

Like with the trickster Oz, your fears are real, but they are not fact. Admittedly, struggling with your father's awkward steps set up your fears, which is why, from your first puppy-love crush to your most recent affair, your choices have trickled down from how your 1st Prince Charming treated you. His messages did not reflect who you were, only who he needed you to believe you were. The power of those messages lies in how they continue to undermine your value as a woman in their profound potential to influence and falsely define your sense of self today. The moment you choose to pull back the curtain you will discover your little girl fears hold only the power you give them.

To become a woman empowered to choose wisely who you date, fall in love with, and if and who you marry, would it be in your best interest to take Toto's example to heart?

If you answer *yes*, then this journey will support you to make a conscious choice to heal your wounded child. Since trust between partners is the essence of a healthy relationship, she will learn she can trust the wise, discerning, and courageous woman you are becoming. With your lead, the two of you will heal each other, and in wholeness you will find the one you long for.

> *It takes a lot of courage to release the familiar*
> *and seemingly secure, to embrace the new.*
> *But there is no real security in what is no longer meaningful.*
> *There is more security in the adventurous and exciting,*
> *for in movement there is life,*
> *and in change there is power.*
>
> Alan Cohen

On the next page is a simple exercise that lists words that describe common personality traits. The list includes typical dynamics of the missteps that can happen in a daddy-daughter dance. This exercise invites you to merely peak behind the curtain of that dance. There is no pressure. There are no incorrect answers. Simply connect the words between your column and his that relate to your relationship. Often your first gut reaction will be the most truthful. If helpful, write these connections down in your Journal. Again, trust you, your child within, and take your time.

Note:

Feeling that familiar fear that long ago froze your child's heart may freeze your woman's heart now. Often, only after we allow ourselves to grieve for deep loss can we accept our situation and start to redefine life for ourselves. **If during this exercise you experience any emotional intensity, please stop reading and seek professional support with a therapist you trust.**

DAUGHTER	DADDY
Anxious	Aggressive
Fear of failure	Rigid
Fear of success	Dominating
Low self-esteem	Inconsistent
Pessimistic	Imposing
Non-orgasmic	Unpredictable
Suicidal	Perfectionist
Depressed	Irresponsible
Fragile	Shaming
Critical	Insulting
Resilient	Lying
Body issues	Demeaning
Addictive/Compulsive	Rejecting
Alcoholic	Weak
Sex/Relationship	Promiscuous
Drugs	Offensive
Compulsive shopping	Addicted
Food addictions	Passive/Aggressive
Career	Unpredictable
Education	Explosive
Passive/Aggressive	Dismissive
Guilty	Secretive
Frozen	Controlling
Bored	Manic
Hopeless	Egomaniac
Unworthy	Unforgiving

You gain strength, courage and confidence by every experience
in which you really stop to look fear in the face.
You must do the thing you cannot do.

Eleanor Roosevelt

You are here because you are committed to finding a partner who will love you in the only way you hoped your father would. Facing your fear through daily journaling and answering *What am I pretending not to know?* supports you to have what you have hoped for all of your life. Unlike your sisters raised by true Prince Charming daddies, you will know the power of conquering a paralyzing past. You will dance to your own music and create the life you want. So, one more time, your question is: *Is the prize of your prince worth facing your fears?*

You are innocent.
Your fears are valid, normal, and expected.
You are not alone.

It is understandable that the last thing you want is to unleash a Pandora's Box of memories you'd much prefer to dance from rather than towards. You are not alone in your fear. You live alongside sisters who know what you know as only a violated child can. Literally millions of women have stories with themes that parallel yours in one way or another. They work alongside you in your office, sit next to you in your classes, jog through your neighborhood and jive next to you in your Zumba class. In time, many of them have taken a deep breath, then pulled back that curtain as fast, or as slowly, as they felt safe doing. Because of their courage, today they live the lives they want to live. They decide when to dance and with who and for how long. **And, they so want you to know the life you are living is not your destiny.** They want you to know that you can trust yourself to question and to make choices like a woman instead of accepting naively as a child. Like them, you can learn to trust the music hiding in your soul. Like them, you can learn to dance your way to the music you choose, with or without a partner.

> ***You are a child of the universe, no less than the trees and the stars.***
> ***You have a right to be here.***
> Max Ehrmann ~ Desiderata

Stay here. Stay here to feel your power instead of believing you are and always will be a victim. Stay here and allow your journaling to tell you your truth. Stay here until your heart is at peace and tells you it is time to go on. This is your turning point, so please take all the time you need.

As you shine light on what you have hidden, you gather up all the heartbreak endured by the little girl that is still you. Be gentle with her. Be your own mother. Keep her picture by your bed. Look into her eyes, listen to her heart, and promise her that you will protect and nurture her as you walk hand-in-hand through your journey. You are the woman now. You are all she has, and from the time you left childhood behind, she has hoped for you to remember her.

Note:

The goal of your journey is not closure or completion, forgetting, forgiving or excusing. No, you cannot forget, maybe not even forgive. What you can do, and must do to find the partner your heart longs for, is to complete the dance with your father on your own terms, whether he is here or not.

JOURNEY JOURNALING:

Seven words that describe my earliest memories of my father.

Seven words that describe him when I was 7, 10, 13, 15, 18.

What unmet childhood needs do I project onto men in my life?

What is my father's legacy to me as my first Prince Charming?

What did I feel when he hurt me?

How did I soothe myself?

What do I feel now?

How did I want him to treat me?

Who did I trust when I could not trust him?

MIRROR MAGIC: *I trust you.*

RECOMMENDED READS:

Wounded Woman: Healing the Father-Daughter Relationship by Linda Leonard

Our Fathers, Ourselves: Fathers, Daughters, and the Changing American Family by Dr. Peggy Drexler

Longing for Dad: Father Loss and Its Impact by Beth Erikson The Wounded Woman: Hope and Healing for Those Who Hurt by Steve Stephens

*** *Sliver of Sky* by Barry Lopez (*Harper's Magazine, January 2013;* NPR/WHYY Fresh Air Interview with Terry Gross)

How do we Forgive our Fathers?

How do we forgive our Fathers? Maybe in a dream?
Do we forgive our Fathers for leaving us too often or forever,
when we were little? Maybe for scaring us with unexpected rage
Or making us nervous because there never seemed to be
any rage at all?

Do we forgive our Fathers for marrying or not marrying our Mothers?
For divorcing or not divorcing our Mothers?
Shall we forgive them for their excess of warmth or coldness?

Shall we forgive them for pushes or for shutting doors, for speaking
through walls, or never speaking or never being silent?
Do we forgive our Fathers in our age or in theirs? Or their
deaths, Saying it to them or not saying it?
If we forgive our Fathers, what is left?
Dick Louri

4 "Shoulding" On Your Life?
Confronting the "Celestial Should Committee" Myth

Our job is not to straighten each other out,
but to help each other up.
Neva Cole

Anyone who doesn't make mistakes isn't trying hard enough.
Wess Roberts

I have no regrets. I wouldn't have lived my life the way I did if I was
going to worry about what people were going to say.
Ingrid Bergman

It takes courage to do what you want.
Other people have a lot of plans for you.
Nobody wants you to do what you want to do.
Joseph Campbell

Life is either a daring adventure or nothing at all. Security is mostly
a superstition. It does not exist in nature.
Helen Keller

Our Terms:

TYRANNY: Arbitrary or unrestrained exercise of power;
despotic abuse of authority; oppressive or unjust; undue severity
or harshness.

FREEDOM: Unrestrained, personal liberty; the power to determine
one's own actions; the right to enjoy.

NANCY

Nancy had thought when she turned twenty she would magically gain some self-confidence, and maybe even move out on her own. She had grown up as the youngest child in a rather strict family. As a timid child, she had never questioned why her parents and older siblings always insisted that they knew what was best for her life. In other words, Nancy's family felt free to *should* on her with great gusto.

At twenty-three years of age Nancy had a high school education, a minimum wage job, no boyfriend, and found herself financially and emotionally chained to her family. She was convinced that she really didn't have what it takes to make it on her own. One thing she did know for sure, whatever the situation, Nancy's family had a rule for it because she couldn't be trusted to do the *right* thing. So, when for the first time in her life Nancy went against them all and enrolled in a psychology class at her community college, her family pretty much came unglued.

If a woman does not keep pace with her companions, perhaps it is because she hears a different drummer. Let her step to the music which she hears, however measured or far away.

Henry David Thoreau (paraphrased)

Nancy was halfway through the semester when her professor, a brilliant woman from Sweden, introduced her adoring class to one of the most revolutionary theories of the 20th Century, the *Tyranny of the Shoulds*. Developed by the courageous, enlightened psychiatrist, Karen Horney, this theory describes the plague of living compulsively tormented to obey the *shoulds*.

No person is your friend who demands your silence or denies your right to grow.

Alice Walker

As Nancy listened to the lecture, the countless *shoulds* of her own life flashed before her eyes. For as long as she could remember, her parents and siblings had told her how she should act, how she should dress, and even how she should think. Now, as an adult, when confronted with a choice, Nancy's mind always went straight to her familiar internal rule-based monologue of debating *What **should** I do?*

Later, as she walked home from class, Nancy's mind asked a question she never could have imagined even thinking before: Could this one ever so ordinary word explain how my life never seems like my own? Could saying *no* to *should* mean I would be saying *yes* to the life I really want?

Such a radical thought stunned her right back into her shoulds. Yes, her parents were strict, but she knew they loved her and just wanted what was best for her. She really should feel guilty for being so selfish, so arrogant ~ dare she admit it... so **w-i-c-k-e-d?** After all, who was she to question her parents who quite possibly did know better than she ever could?

> *If one has an accurate conception of themselves,*
> *they are free to realize their potential.*
> Karen Horney, pioneering Feminine Psychologist (1885–1952)

Shoulds have a Crippling Effect
on One's Early Development

Not only are we humans born unaware of what the rules are, we don't have a clue that there even are any rules. We each just enter this wonderful world as a free fresh spirit with a biological desperation to be safe and nurtured. Nurturing most definitely includes endless opportunities to play and imagine as our parents watch on, eager to discover *Who is this little child of mine?*

The trouble starts when the stork drops a baby into a family like Nancy's. All of the child's innate curiosity is crushed under rules that stifle her own unique little person. Rather than learning how to make mistakes or practical choices, parents expect her to conform to their rigid expectations, sometimes from day one!

In such a restrictive environment, rather than the child's personality being allowed to blossom, her authentic self is buried underneath the parent's insistence on compliance. So young, she learns that being loved is the reward for being *good*, as in being who you are expected to be. If you follow all the *shoulds*, then you will be perfect enough to earn love. How can an innocent little child possibly know that what her parents expect is impossible? She is just a kid looking for some hugs and kisses. She can't know she has to be perfect to earn them.

The Celestial Should Committee

If you were raised to comply with a list of *shoulds*, now as a woman demands to be compliant likely feel normal, even comfortable to you now. When your friends, family or lover dictate your decisions, your childhood messages have already set you up to readily meet their agenda, not yours.

Where did all of these *shoulds* come from? Could it be that somewhere out there exists a grand *Celestial Should Committee* ~ the Supreme Court of Cosmic Consciousness? And, how great is that? Because you are too naive to figure out the correct response to every possible life situation, the *Should Committee* has conveniently pre-determined how you should act, think, and respond to all one million of them. You just need to turn off your intuition and intelligence, and comply with what others tell you to think and do. Of course, there is a problem with this. When you resign your life to the agendas of others ~ who truly cannot possibly know you better than you know yourself ~ the authentic life will never be yours.

Perfectionism is the voice of the oppressor, the enemy of the people.
It will keep you insane your whole life.
Anne Lamott

When you feel driven to be *perfect*, as in meet all of the demands of the *Should Committee*, you make the choice to live by rigid adherence to others' ideas. What's more, even though you may already be doing a fabulous job of *shoulding* on your life, chances are there still is at least one other someone who gallantly takes charge of the enormous task of ensuring you stay on the *right* way, and for your own good. You know who it is... that parent, sibling, friend, co-worker, boss, girlfriend, boyfriend or lover who genuinely believes it is their role in life to tell you how to live yours.

Known as C-O-N-T-R-O-L-L-E-R-S, these self-appointed members of the *Celestial Should Committee* consider it their moral obligation to keep you on the straight and narrow. What a one sided deal! With your permission, they make you feel guilty for not being *perfect* according to how they define *perfect*.

CONTROLLERS believe you should:

- Be the epitome of generosity and unselfishness

- Be the perfect lover, friend, parent, employee, etc.

- Be able to endure any hardship & solve every problem

- Be totally competent

- Be self-reliant

- Know, understand and foresee everything

- Put others' needs before your own

- Protect your family from pain

- Never feel angry or jealous

- Never make mistakes

- Never complain

- Never be tired or sick

- Never be afraid

- Never feel sexually attracted to certain people

- Never feel hurt; always feel happy and serene

- Never take time for your own pleasure

Oh, and also…You *Should*:

- Forgive unconditionally

- Love unconditionally

- Deny your truth if it's inconvenient to the *Should Committee*

> ***Hell is getting to the end of your life,***
> ***and discovering you had choices.***
> Soren Kierkegaard

Should is a sham that shackles you to another's ego-driven idea that you should be the *good* girl rather than the real woman you are. The *Shoulds* are as crippling to your freedom to live freely as paralysis is to your freedom to move freely. That's the irony. No one would choose paralysis, yet so many of us raised with the *shoulds* are paralyzed by the fear of being imperfect. And what do we call people who think they are one of the rare few willing to make the sacrifices to be perfect? Maybe superficial? Maybe self-absorbed? Maybe naïve? Maybe it's time to consider a better way than what everyone else has in mind for your life.

When you are about to think or say that crippling word, try just saying *No*. This will take some practice, but your reward will be trading tyranny for freedom.

> **To go against the dominant thinking of your friend,**
> **or of most of the people you see every day, is perhaps**
> **the most difficult act of heroism you can perform.**
> Theodore White

In her book, *Don't Push the River,* author Barry Stevens shares her idea for transferring allegiance from the *Should Committee* to the one you can truly trust. Rather than rushing to judge yourself as inadequate, stupid, guilty or unworthy as to what you should have said, or how you should have felt, thought, or acted, Stevens offers the concept of the **Gentle Observer**.

My image of the *Gentle Observer* comes from the Muppet Show. Statler and Waldorf are those two crazy old men looking down from the balcony as they make comments about what's happening on the stage below. I'm not sure how gentle they are, but they are definitely observant. For our purposes, imagine if you took their example and removed yourself from all of the drama going on down there on the stage of your life. Instead, you're sitting up there in the balcony with Statler and Waldorf, removed from all the craziness. As you observe each situation, you simply note, *Oh, so when that happens in my life, this is how I respond. Mmmm. Interesting, isn't it?* Upon reflection and without a hint of guilt, you may consider *Would giving or receiving forgiveness settle my soul? Did my action or reaction serve me or not?* If not, you may think how you might shift your response in the future. But, notice not once do you judge your response. You are simply being your own *Gentle Observer*.

> ### *Power is the ability not to have to please.*
> Elizabeth Janeway

So, what's next? Well, perhaps a Mirror Magic moment to discuss firing your personal *Should Committee*? For instance, you could give a simple, sincere response the next time they try *shoulding*, such as *Why, thank you for sharing*, or *I'll consider that option*, or *You know, I've decided to decide for myself.* What happens when your *shoulds* and *should nots* transform into *What do I want?* or *What choice serves me?* Whatever you want!

One word of caution: As you begin to exercise your new found *attitude*, you will threaten those who relish the power of *shoulding* on your life. Prepare for resistance because when you take control of your life your empowered choice reveals their insecurities, and may even unravel their reason for living. And, since you have historically given them permission to do so, be prepared when they don't appreciate you dethroning them from their perch. Just try disempowering them without getting their knickers all tied up in knots, because the truth is they need you to believe they know best... desperately.

> ### *Everything rights itself. That's why it doesn't matter if I do something wrong. It's trying not to make mistakes and trying to correct them that louses me up.*
> Barry Stevens, Gestalt Therapist

Even though you may have been told otherwise, you hold within you the wisdom to know and choose the path that leads you to love and the life you long for. To prove it, think back on the major decisions you have made in your life. Which choices were you talked into, and which choices did you make regardless of anyone else's opinion? For many of us, the decisions we made by trusting our intuition are the decisions we don't regret. Even if the consequences were not all that we hoped for, we still feel peace for we chose what we believed would serve our goals, our hopes and our dreams. Those decisions that we were talked into, or forced into *for our own good...* chances are we regret greatly.

For Review:

What the *Celestial Should Committee* needs you to believe:

- Every possible life situation has been examined.
- In every imaginable situation, there is a proper way to feel, think, and act.
- To be a good girl, you must think, feel and act in accordance with what they dictate.

How to Confront the Celestial Should Committee:

- What would I prefer/need/want in this situation?
- What serves/pleases me in this situation?
- Who am I in this situation?

> *It took me a long time not to judge myself*
> *through someone else's eyes.*
> Sally Field

In the weeks following the lecture, Nancy made a list of the *shoulds* from her childhood. Then, she made another list of how those *shoulds* had wormed their way into her adult life. Then, she journaled her answers to the following questions:

JOURNEY JOURNALING:

What *shoulds* of childhood do I remember?

Who was invested in *shoulding on* me, and in what situations?

If these voices are still in my life, how do I quiet them?

What do I believe are their motives for *shoulding* on my life?

What legitimate guidance has my *Should Committee* provided?

How have the *shoulds* impacted my adult life?

What are the *shoulds* that I now reject?

What choices will I make to serve my best interests?

What are the decisions I have made on my own with no regret?

What will change in my life when I just say NO to *shoulds*?

MIRROR MAGIC: *I trust you.*

RECOMMENDED READS:

The Women's Book of Empowerment: 323 Affirmations that Change Everyday Problems into Moments of Potential by Charlene M. Proctor, Ph.D.

Let Your Goddess Grow! 7 Spiritual Lessons on Female Power and Positive Thinking by Charlene M. Proctor, Ph.D.

The Dance: Moving to the Rhythms of Your True Self by Oriah Mountain Dreamer Harper

The Woman's Handbook for Self-Empowerment by Linda Ellis Eastman

5 *Into Your Intuition:*
When in Doubt, Trust Your Tummy

Trust yourself. You know more than you think you do.
Benjamin Spock

I feel there are two people inside me, me and my intuition. If I go against her, she'll screw me every time. If I follow her, we get along quite nicely. Kim Bassinger

Intuition is always right in at least two important ways: 1.) It is always in response to something. 2.) It always has your best interest at heart. Unlike worry, it will not waste your time.
Gavin De Becker, *The Gift of Fear*

Our Terms:

INTUITION: From the Latin word *Intueri*, meaning to look within; the power or facility of attaining direct knowledge without evidence of rational thought.

TRUST: To depend upon; reliance on the integrity, strength, ability, surety of a person or thing; committing to one's care for safe keeping.

CLAIRE

At last, Claire's wedding was only two weeks away! Her bridal shower was this weekend, and her girlfriends were beside themselves with happiness for her. They had all been married at least three years, and now it was Claire's turn to marry her handsome groom. The wedding was going to be beautiful. Claire had invited seven of her closest friends and family to be her bridesmaids, including her baby sister and Ted's twin sister. She'd picked just the right color green for their dresses, and they were gorgeous. The ceremony would be held in her childhood church, and her grandfather was officiating. Family was flying in from both coasts, as well as Canada, and every bit of Claire's life was pretty much a whirlwind counting down the days.

When she did manage a few quiet moments to herself, Claire's mental monologue went something like this: *When I picture myself walking down the aisle towards him, I can feel my gut screaming 'NO!' But, I'm twenty-eight years old, and no one else has ever come close to proposing until Ted. What if he's really the only one that will ever ask me? What if this is my only chance to be married and have the children I've always wanted? He makes decent money, and the idea of me working for the rest of my life scares me to death. I can't always think like a little girl with the perfect fantasy coming true. I have to be practical. I'm OK with his boys' nights out, and his working long hours. After all, we're saving for our home, and every hour he works is paying for our down payment. I'll be fine. Once the wedding is over, and we're on our honeymoon, I'll feel… I'll know I made the right choice. Really. I'm just having those jitters that everyone talks about. And, if I really truly have made a mistake, I can get divorced. So many of my friends have.*

When a man doesn't absolutely positively feel like your Beloved, your gut will ring the alarm bells to stop those wedding bells, or whatever other horrible decision you're about to regret. If, on the other hand, you are in tune with your value, your purpose and your integrity, your courage will come forward to change your course. Yes, that can mean keeping absolutely silent when the moment comes to answer *I do*. Yes, even if you are standing there wearing the most beautiful bridal gown of all time as you look into the handsome face of your intended groom. If your gut is screaming *NO!*… for your own sweet sake **trust it**, because if you choose in that fateful moment to ignore the knot in your gut by tying the knot in your life with the wrong man, your choice will bring pain that will wrench you for years to come.

Of course, trusting your intuition applies to all of life's situations, whether seemingly insignificant or not. What decision are you debating right now? If your mind is going into meltdown trying to make an important choice, then turn off all the craziness in your head, and turn instead into your intuition. Be still. Pay attention. What is your body telling you? What feelings are there? If ever you are honest with yourself, this is the time.

JESSICA

Jessica had just accepted a promotion to Director of Human Resources of a major corporation. The position required a transfer to the Corporate Headquarters, located 500 hundred miles away from her hometown. She was so ready for the big city life, and earning the salary to pay for it! Always an *I can do it myself* woman, within a week Jessica had already organized her office, leased a convertible, and bought a luxury condo with a view of the river. At this particular moment, she was tackling moving boxes into the elevator when a man saw her struggle and stepped in to offer his help. Instantly, Jessica felt her stomach tighten. Even though he was wearing a sport shirt and slacks, there was something eerie about his eyes, and the sound of his voice. With her most powerful feminine intuition sounding alarm bells, intelligent, successful Jessica ignored every scary sensation her body was sending her as she rationalized that no one in this building could be dangerous. An hour later, bruised and bleeding, she crawled to her purse, pulled out her cell phone, then screamed to the 911 operator *Help me! I've been raped!*

> *We get a signal prior to violence. There are pre-incident indicators that happen before violence occurs.*
> Gavin De Becker

When animals sense danger they use their natural instincts to protect themselves. Some run, some fly, some climb trees, some change color to blend in with their environment. Ah, but take a smart woman sensing danger and all bets are off. We've all been there. Looking potential danger right in the eye, all sorts of ideas pop into our heads to override the *creepy* factor that's crawling up the back of our necks. And, let's face it, the vast majority of the time when our tummies tighten, it's we girls who think *I've got to be nice. I don't want him to think I'm not nice.* And so we allow a potential rapist, or worse, into our vulnerability when there's not another animal in nature that would even consider it.

Maybe the animal kingdom has the advantage here because, unlike ours, their brains lack the ability to debate when in danger. They smell danger and don't wait around to find out why. But, just our luck, the human brain has two hemispheres. Our left brain **thinks**. It's focused in time and space. It is rational, logical and processes step by step. Our right brain **feels**. It taps into the part of our mind that has no sense of time or space. It instantly senses environmental cues, our emotions, and what we see, hear, touch, taste and smell. In a nanosecond, it analyzes the whole situation, then sends us signals **for our own protection!** In other words, the right brain is a girl's best friend.

Did you know? Every two minutes, a woman in the U.S. is sexually assaulted. Two thirds of assaults are committed by someone known to the victim. To compound the threat, over 97% of rapists will never spend more than a day in jail. Author Gavin de Becker warns women of men:

- Who act too friendly
- Who give too much information
- Who joke to get your attention
- Who help you, then expect you to return the favor
- Who say I promise I won't call you, then call you
- Who won't accept *no* when you tell them *NO!*

In our narcissistic world, just being a woman puts you in profound risk of becoming prey to some sick mind. Violence against women has become so common place we hardly stop to notice when headlines report women missing from their campuses, their work places, their cars, their jogging trails, their neighborhood malls and their homes. Only a bimbo would fail to see how vulnerable we are as women, and the danger only increases when we fail to trust our own intuitive knowing.

In the original Latin, <u>INTELLIGENCE</u> and <u>INTUITION</u> share the same root: Of EQUAL Value

Even though many modern cultures value thinking over feeling, intuition is often more accurate than logic when your emotional or physical safety is at stake. Your intuition instantly warns you of *Danger Ahead!* as in whether to step into that elevator, accept an offer of help, stay with a man or put on your tennies and run like hell!

Ever notice the knot in your tummy when you doubt your date's story about why he was late? What happens to that knot when you later discover he doesn't share your core values and you fall in love with him anyway? What do you feel when your intuition is screaming *NO! This isn't what you want,* while you keep quiet about your thoughts and feelings, because evidently sharing them honestly makes him unhappy? Of course, when those issues come up, whether the two of you argue or not, your private inner battle rages as your logical left brain debates with your intuitive right brain as to how important living your truth really is. Are you willing to silence your voice to keep a man you ultimately have little or nothing in common with, or worse…are afraid of? Do you not only devalue yourself in your eyes, but in his when you ignore those warnings just to keep the relationship going? Is giving up your happiness to a man who doesn't make you happy really worth such sacrifice?

When your inner voice whispers *Just tell him 'I'm sorry, so sorry, but I've changed my mind. I don't want to date you / sleep with you / marry you / lend you money'*… please pay attention. You don't have to eliminate rational thought, just recognize its limitations, especially in any situation where you are vulnerable. And again, let's be honest. You're a woman. You are vulnerable.

Your intuition is there to protect you. Before you journal, I encourage you to take a few days to practice *feeling* the signals your intuition sends you. Compare the emotions you *sense* when you are in conversation with friends, associates, or strangers. Pay attention to simple everyday events like your *sense* of the person taking your order behind the counter. Bring into awareness what your inner knowing has known all along: your instincts are working overtime to keep you safe in the world around you.

JOURNEY JOURNALING:

What is my gut feeling about trusting my intuition?

Where in my body do I feel fear?

What happened the last time I trusted/didn't trust my intuition?

What are my most vulnerable places and activities?

What intuitive choices do I already make for self-protection?

What am I going to do to strengthen my immediate response in a vulnerable situation?

MIRROR MAGIC: *I trust you.*

RECOMMENDED READS:

Awakening Intuition: Using Your Mind-Body Network for In sight and Healing by Mona Lisa Schulz M.D. Ph.D. and Christiane Northrup M.D. (Apr 20, 1999)

BLINK – The Power of Thinking Without Thinking by Malcolm Gladwell (best-selling author of *The Tipping Point*)

The Gift of FEAR and Other Survival Signals that Protect Us from Violence by Gavin De Becker

6 *The Choice Is Always Yours:*
A Parable of Power

Whenever I have to choose between two evils, I always like
to try the one I haven't tried before.
Mae West

When we walk to the end of all the light we have, and take a step
into the darkness of the unknown, we must believe one of two things
will happen: that we will land on something solid,
or we will learn to fly.
Unknown

Our Terms:

CHOOSE: To select from a number of possibilities; to pick by preference; to want or desire, as one thing over another.

CHOICE: An act or instance of choosing; the right, power, or opportunity to choose; option; worthy of being chosen; excellent; superior; carefully selected; the best part.

FEAR: A distressing emotion aroused by impending danger, evil, or pain, whether the threat is real or imagined; concern or anxiety; be afraid of; dread; worry.

OBLIGATION: Bound by a sense of duty; a binding promise.

GUILT: Feeling of remorse or responsibility for some offense, whether real or imagined.

JOY: A feeling or state of great delight or rejoicing; happiness; elation; the expression or display of gaiety

Any meaningful choice is driven by one of two options Do you choose to avoid pain and have pleasure? Or, do you avoid pleasure and have pain? The choices you make move your life forward or hold your life back.

According to psychotherapist Susan Forward, the pain choice is made from the place of **FOG** (**F**ear, **O**bligation and **G**uilt).

The pleasure choice is made from the desire for **JOY** (the Joy-Of-**Y**es). The bridge between Fog and Joy is called *Truth*. The river it crosses is called *Life,* which flows on no matter if you cross the bridge or not. The BRIDGE is always there. It is in front of you now.

If one chooses to remain in the FOG, the emotions of fear, obligation and guilt multiply, making the FOG more dense. Sometimes the FOG becomes so dense that people have been known to lose sight of the bridge. They need great help to find it again, if they make that choice. Some have remained in the FOG so long they have forgotten there ever was a bridge at all.

If one chooses to remain in JOY, the pleasure of the clear sky warms their body and delights their mind. From the sunny side of the river one can see the FOG on the other side. Those on this side often decide that only a fool would leave the pleasure of JOY to return to the cold dampness of the FOG. Some have remained in the JOY so long they have forgotten there ever was a bridge at all.

The choice to WAIT to make a choice is also based on your choice to live in FOG or to live in JOY. If you choose not to cross the bridge today, your crossing will be more difficult and complicated tomorrow. The act of deliberation has been known to last a moment or an entire lifetime. Once the choice is made, one's crossing may happen in the blink of an eye.

> ***Respect yourself enough to walk away from anything that no longer serves you, grows you, or makes you happy.***
> Anonymous

JOURNEY JOURNALING:

What side of the bridge did my life begin on?

What side of the bridge am I on today?

What life circumstances brought me to this side?

What personal choices keep me here?

How long do I intend to stay on this side of the bridge?

What serves me about being on this side of the bridge?

Who do I know who lives in the FOG?

Who do I know who lives in JOY?

MIRROR MAGIC: *Fog or Joy?*

RECOMMENDED READS:

Emotional Blackmail: When the People in Your Life Use Fear, Obligation and Guilt to Manipulate You by Susan Forward

Toxic Parents: Overcoming Their Hurtful Legacy and Reclaiming Your Life by Craig Buck

The Dance of Anger: A Woman's Guide to Changing the Patterns in Intimate Relationships by Harriet Lerner, Ph.D.

7 *The Power of Your Words:*
She~Brain at the Ready

Our Terms:

WORD: A unit of language that conveys meaning; verbal expression, as in expressing one's emotions in words.

POWER: Ability to do or act; authority to exercise influence on others.

RITA

Rita was the baby of the family. She had three older brothers she always hoped would act like every little girl's dream of being her protectors. Actually, only Joey, the eldest, was the one she knew would always have her back. Born with an exceptionally timid personality, even as a toddler, Rita's words were few and far between. She knew she could count on her big brother Joey to speak for her as if he could read her mind. It wasn't that she couldn't talk. She just didn't know what to say, so he would encourage her. Often he suggested, *Let's make up a story, Rita,* and they would.

She trusted Joey more than anyone. She could tell him her secrets and little girl wishes because Joey would keep them safe. Over the years her twin brothers, Ken and Steven, just grew impatient with her *lack of spunk,* as they called it. *Just say what you want, Rita!* or *We can't hear you, Rita!* they would shout in her face. That didn't make it any easier for her.

To no one's surprise, Rita grew up to act as if what she wanted didn't matter. She always asked permission. She was always compliant. At school, she offered the same opinions as her classmates. She rarely looked someone in the eye. She even apologized for things she hadn't done. By her eighteenth birthday the majority of Joey's time and energy revolved around keeping his little sister away from high school *losers* who smelled easy prey. Ken and Steven had long since given up. After all, what did she expect when her favorite phrases were *I don't know how, I just don't know,* or *What should I do?* Couldn't she see her dead end life was her fault if she wouldn't speak up for herself?

In Chapter 2, you learned the power of speaking your truth. This chapter targets the power of how you say it.

Your Words have Power

The enormous power of words lies in the *meaning* they trigger within the brain because words have the power to activate your memories, emotions, actions, thoughts and ideas. The words you choose have the power to tell people who you are, and how you expect to be treated. Your words have the power to build people up and give them pleasure, or rob them of pleasure and cause great pain.

When people speak face-to-face, their personalities, tone of voice, and body language affect the listener. In contrast, written words are devoid of a speaker's energy. Basically, they are simply black symbols printed on a white page.

Even so, notice what feelings the following words generate:

You're so smart.	You're so stupid.
You can do anything.	You can't do anything.
You're capable.	You're incapable.

As you just read the words in each column, without any thought of what each meant, or who might say them, their power immediately woke up your emotions. The positive words in the left column tuned into your *happy place*; those in the right column tuned into your *pain*. For both columns, your intuition likely tuned into any history that you may have with each phrase. That's the power of words ~ even on a page.

What is your emotional response to each of the following?

You should. You must. You ought.

Could you? Would you? May we? Perhaps?

I can't. I hope. If only. Tell me what to do.

What do you think? I made a mistake. I'm sorry.

Which of the following match with which word group above?

Convey both confidence and humility

Cause resistance to whatever comes next

Project powerlessness and learned helplessness

Invite opportunities for agreement, cooperation, and choice

Does a Powerful Woman use Weak Words?

When a woman doubts her value, even if she doesn't say it, she can give up her power by reclaiming her childhood's language of helplessness, apology and submission. When she uses such disempowering phrases such as *Can I? Will you let me? I can't,* and the now infamous *I don't know*, she not only projects herself as weak, she also puts herself at risk to a man seeking power and control. Such a man will interpret her weak words as permission to treat her as the immature child she presents herself to be. Which of the phrases below are most typical of the words you use in relating to a partner?

HELPLESSNESS	POWER
I can't	I won't
I should	I could
I hope	I know
If only	Next time
It's not my fault	I'm responsible
It's a problem	It's an opportunity
What will I do?	I can handle it
Life's a struggle	Life's an adventure

Narcissistic men are masters at sniffing out a vulnerable woman, and often her words give him his first clues. Just by listening he can learn more about her than she knows about herself. Recognizing the potential to meet his obsessive need for power, such a man will use **his** words to manipulate this unsuspecting, naive woman into an inequitable relationship. To snare her, he will use his words to sound so logical, so reasonable that she fails to see he is taking control to take her down as he challenges her thinking, her beliefs and her actions. If she ignores those alarm bells clanging in her brain, she hands her power to the manipulative power of his words. Hardly a fair trade, don't you think?

> **People treat you the way you train them to treat you.**
> Martin Rutte

When you claim the power of your words, you train your brain to speak for the woman you are. Words such as *I will, I won't* and *I'm responsible* build the scaffolding for your power platform. Especially in an intimate relationship, *NaughtABimbeaux* knows a man treats her the way she trains him to treat her. She chooses words that make it clear that she expects and only accepts fairness, flexibility and mutual respect in their relationship.

A Word about BULLYING:

> **Sticks and Stones may break my bones,**
> **but words will never hurt me.**

Parents and teachers often use that phrase when a child is hurt by another's words. It may help the adults feel that they've done their job, but unfortunately it is far from true. Words meant to insult, demoralize, and dehumanize in childhood can last a lifetime in the brain of the bullied child.

If you were a victim of verbal violence, those tapes can still play in your sub-conscious brain. If those cruel messages came from the lips of your parents, their impact was even more profound to the development of who you believe you are today. If those same words were followed by contradictory assurances, such as *I'm saying this for your own good* or *Because I love you*, you grew up in an impossible *double bind* dilemma ~ being *torn down* at the same time you were being *built up*.

> **Yelling at living things does tend to kill the spirit in them.**
> **Sticks and stones won't break our bones,**
> **but words will break our hearts.**
>
> Robert Fulghum

Whether from the lips of a child or an adult, harsh and unjustified words can live on in your endless self-judgment, and in your tendency to self-sabotage your own goals. It can take as little as one episode of hearing yourself called derogatory names to believe ~ for the rest of your life ~ those hateful words are true, that you *are dumb, ugly, stupid, spoiled, lazy, unforgiving, undeserving, worthless.*

When you have an experience that triggers any of these lies, you may once again feel that stabbing pain in your heart. And, as for many of us, you may interpret that pain as validation of your childhood belief, *See, they were right.* Still believing the lie, you become your own critic, devaluing your own worth with your own voice. Then, you live at the mercy of feelings that control your emotions and choices without even being aware, as you recycle your family dysfunction and *prove* to those who should matter that they were right all along about you.

> **The way we talk to our children**
> **becomes their inner voice.**
>
> Peggy O'Mara

In previous chapters, several of our sisters' stories shared how their courage to love themselves broke the horror of their family's cycle of violence. Like them, are you ready to accept that you have full rights to your righteous rage for what was done to you? Like them, will you break the cycle?

JOURNEY JOURNALING:

What hurtful words do I remember spoken to me?

How old was I and what did I feel when I heard them?

Who listened and gave me compassion?

Who do I respect because of the way they speak to me or others?

Who do I not respect because of the way they speak to me or others?

What recent situation may have had a more positive outcome if I had spoken with invitation rather than obstruction?

MIRROR MAGIC: *It wasn't true.*

RECOMMENDED READS:

The Verbally Abusive Relationship: How to Recognize it and How to Respond by Patricia Evans

Victory over Verbal Abuse: A Healing Guide to Renewing Your Spirit and Reclaiming Your Life by Patricia Evans

Toxic Parents: Overcoming Their Hurtful Legacy and Reclaiming Your Life by Susan Forward

She stood in the storm, and when the wind did not blow her way, she adjusted her sails.
Elizabeth Edwards

8 Sisterhood:
Holding You UP When You're Falling Down

To be one woman, truly, wholly, is to be all women.
Kate Braverman

Both within the family and without, our sisters hold up the mirror of who we are and of who we can dare to become.
Elizabeth Fishel

'You have been my friends,' replied Charlotte.
'That in itself is a tremendous thing.'
E.B. White

Nobody sees a flower really; it is so small. We haven't time, and to see takes time ~ like to have a friend takes time.
Georgia O'Keefe

Our Terms:

FRIEND: A person attached to another by feelings of affection or personal regard; a person who gives assistance; a person who is on good terms with another; a person who is not hostile.

SISTER: A female offspring having both parents in common with another offspring; female friend or protector regarded as a sister; half-sister, female offspring having only one parent in common with another offspring.

SISTERHOOD: The state of being a sister; a group of sisters; women with a common interest, as in social, charitable, business or political purposes; congenial relationship or companionship among women; mutual female esteem, concern, and support.

JOY

Joy was the fourth in a family of five children ~ two sons and three daughters. Just before her eighth birthday, playing fetch with her dog in the front yard, Joy impulsively ran into the street after the ball. In that moment, she was hit by a speeding motorcycle as it ran over her left leg. When her father heard her screams he came running and found her leg almost severed. She was in shock, and bleeding to death. In the emergency room Joy required six times the amount of an adult transfusion. Holding onto hope, her parents were devastated when the doctors came through the surgery doors to tell them they could not stop the hemorrhaging. They could not save their daughter.

It was Joy's father who could not accept such devastating news. It was his terrified insistence that sent the surgeons back into the operating room. Surely it was a miracle when, after another hour, the hemorrhaging had stopped. Joy's heart was beating strong enough to keep her alive. Miraculously, they were able to reattach her leg.

The results of her injuries required several more surgeries, and three years to regain her mobility. When not in the hospital, therapists came to their home three days a week. Her parents hired a teacher who came daily to keep her education on track. Friends and family often stopped by to check on her progress and wish her well. Everyone told her, *Joy, you are such a brave little soldier!* Everyone except for her younger sister, that is.

Cheryl was crazed with jealousy. Despite Joy's earlier efforts to be close to her younger sister, after the accident Cheryl was relentless in making her sister's situation worse. If their mother told Cheryl to bring lunch to her sister, she would knock it off the tray and blame the spilled milk on Joy. When Joy was learning how to walk with crutches, Cheryl would *accidentally* bump into her, sending her crashing to the floor. Cheryl was always the first one to meet the mailman at their door. You can be sure if *Joy* was on the envelope, it disappeared before anyone saw it.

After four years, fully recovered and back in school, Joy hoped *Maybe now that I'm not getting so much attention, Cheryl and I can be close.* But, that was not to be. Cheryl became even more passive-aggressive, and by the time they were in high school, though living under the same roof, their hearts and lives had gone in separate ways.

After graduating from college, Joy was to marry and, from the goodness of her heart, she asked Cheryl to be her bridesmaid. She accepted, yet the night before the wedding Cheryl felt compelled to come into Joy's bedroom to announce, *You know I've always hated you.* Joy could only nod in agreement.

> *The desire to be and have a sister is a primitive and profound one that may have everything or nothing to do with the family a woman is born to. It is a desire to know and be known by someone who shares blood and body, history and dreams, the darkest secrets and the glassiest beads of truth.*
> Elizabeth Fishel

Joy's adult life has been filled with the love of sisters who are of her heart, if not her biology. Her childhood friend, Lindy, has fulfilled all that sisters are created to be. Although living on opposite coasts, and holding to opposite opinions about politics and religion, the rare times they do share by texting, phone calls or *live and in person*, it is as if they've not been apart one single day ever. They still laugh about the day they pricked their fingers with pins, then mingled their drops of blood, and buried the pins with tiny Bibles in Joy's backyard for their *Blood Sisters* ritual.

Lindy knows the back story of Joy's family. She remembers Cheryl's attempts to hurt Joy when she was most vulnerable. She remembers how funny and charismatic Joy's daddy was, and how much he loved her. But, what makes them true sisters is that there is nothing either could do or say that would compromise the trust and respect that holds their hearts together. Near or far, young or getting older, they are each other's *safe place* ~ today, tomorrow, and forever.

> **Sisterhood is the essence of all the wisdom of the ages,**
> **distilled into a single word. You cannot see sisterhood, neither can**
> **you hear it nor taste it. But you can feel it a hundred times a day.**
> **It is a pat on the back, a smile of encouragement.**
> **It's someone to share with, to celebrate your achievements.**
> A Wise Woman

How does sisterhood find its way into a book about finding Prince Charming? No, it has nothing to do with those evil, beady eyed stepsisters. The true sisterhood has everything to do with our shared knowing that not just frogs, but even one's prince will not arrive equipped to fully understand the depth of all we intuitively know, feel and long for as women. (Much more about that in Chapter 15).

The intuitive knowing of women transcends history, culture, and is woven into every cell of our bodies. From the ancient days of women gathering around the water well to today's International Women's Conferences, the world of men observes the world of women with curiosity, sometimes respect, often fear, and always with wonder. Our friendships not only shape who we are and who we become, they soothe our tumultuous inner world, fill the emotional gaps in our relationships with men, and help us remember who we really are.

> *You said good friends are hard to come by. I laughed and*
> *bought you a beer 'cause it's too corny to cry.*
> Indigo Girls

Tend and Befriend

For over five decades, psychological research told us that in stressful situations, both men and women rely on the *fight or flight* response to escape danger. These male-centered studies claimed that for both genders our options were to become aggressive to protect ourselves, or emotionally and/or physically withdraw from the stressful situation. Now, researchers suspect we women share a larger behavioral repertoire than just *fight or flight*.

While men most often react with the fight or flight response, in 2000, stunning research (by women) found this *one option fits all* to not be true. For males, the release of testosterone increases when they are under stress, hence their fight or flight response.

When we of the sisterhood feel stressed within, our bodies make chemicals that cause us to seek other women to support and nurture each other, including the most vulnerable among us. The hormone *oxytocin* buffers our fight or flight response while increasing our innate tendency to protect children, and gather with other women, thus giving us a sense of calm and relaxation. Rather than the panic of fight or flight, our innate response is to find peace as we *tend and befriend*.

Discovering that we respond to stress differently than men began in an Aha! moment by two women scientists as they discussed their findings in a lab at UCLA. *We joked that when the women who worked in the lab were stressed, they came in, cleaned the lab, had coffee, and bonded*, says Dr. Laura Cousin Klein, Ph.D., Assistant Professor of Bio- Behavioral Health at Penn State University. When the men were stressed, they fled to their offices, shut the doors, and turned off their phones.

Until their study was published, scientists generally believed that when people experience stress, they trigger a hormonal cascade that revs the body to either stand and fight or flee, as fast as possible. It's an ancient survival mechanism left over from the time we were chased across the planet by scary creatures, such as saber-toothed tigers or men gone wild!

It all started when Dr. Klein commented one day to fellow researcher Shelley Taylor that nearly 90% of the stress research was on males. She showed her data from her lab, and the two knew instantly that they were onto something!

Taylor and Klein cleared their schedules and started meeting with scientists from related fields. They soon discovered that by not including women in stress research, scientists had made a huge mistake. Dr. Klein noted, *The fact that women respond to stress differently than men has significant implications for our health. It may take some time for new studies to reveal all the ways that oxytocin encourages us to care for children and hang out with other women, but the 'tend and befriend' notion may explain why women consistently outlive men.*

Because of this research, we now know that females of many species respond to stressful conditions, not by fighting and fleeing, but by protecting and nurturing their young (the *tend* response), and by seeking to gather together in social contact and support from others ~ especially other females (the *befriend* response).

Listening is a magnetic and strange thing, a creative force.
The friends who listen to us are the ones we move toward. When
we are listened to, it creates us, it makes us unfold and expand.
Karl Menninger

Why Do Women Lives an Average of
7 ½ Years Longer than Men?

Study after study, such as the one found at WomensHeart.org, has found that social ties reduce our risk of disease by lowering our blood pressure, heart rate and cholesterol. *There's no doubt,* says Dr. Klein, *that friends are helping us live longer.*

Research supports that the *tend-and-befriend* pattern exhibited by women probably evolved through natural selection. Thousands of generations ago, fleeing or fighting in stressful situations were not viable options for a female who was pregnant, or taking care of off-spring. In their best interest, women who developed and maintained social alliances were better able to care for multiple offspring in stressful times, and thus survive.

In this 21st century, female companionship is also helping women live better. The famed Harvard Medical School's Nurses' Health Study found that the more friends women have the less likely we are to develop physical impairments or disease as we age. Having strong friendships also means we are more likely to pursue options that give us more fulfilling lives. The researchers concluded that not having close friends is as detrimental to our health as smoking or carrying extra weight.

Real friends are those who, when you've made a fool of yourself, don't feel that you've done a permanent job.
Erwin T. Randall

Other research, such as a study recently published in *Men's Health Magazine,* indicates that men are more likely to respond to stressful experiences by developing certain stress-related disorders, including hypertension, ulcers, aggressive behavior, or abuse of alcohol or hard drugs. Men's brains, as we shall see in Chapter 15, are wired as almost polar opposites to ours.

You are well aware that men comprehend, think, feel, and process so differently than we do. To complicate matters, under stress, a man's fight or flight options run the gamut of flipping on the nearest sports' channel or starting an argument with the woman giving them all this stress! Those are typical of the options that pop into their heads. Can you imagine the testosterone rush those adorable creatures get when we beg, *Honey, let's talk about this,* or *Let's work on our relationship?* No wonder they're running for their man caves!

When a single, eager female starts coming on too strong to a clue-less male ~ ready to rope him in, wrap him up and take him home ~ what else can he do but flee to his man cave to quiet his testosterone tizzy? So, let's say she actually manages to pull him out of his cave and drag him home. Have you ever known a woman who, after *catching* a new man, eagerly abandoned her girlfriends? Was her withdrawal because she tried to melt her life into his because she believed he could fulfill her craving for emotional intimacy as well as any female? Did she think he would leave behind all vestiges of masculine bonding to be at the beck and call of one woman, namely her? Did she honestly think he could replace the camaraderie of her BFF sisters? Oh dear!

Hold a true friend with both your hands.
Nigerian Proverb

As the above research shows, and our hearts know, it is our sisters who sustain our physical and emotional health, whether we are in or out of romantic relationships. Many of us were blessed at birth with biological sisters who became our best friends. Many of us weren't. For the sake of your physical and mental health, if your biological sisters treated you more like Cinderella's step-sisters than a true friend, you can choose sisters who don't happen to share your DNA, but who do share your heart. In fact, like Joy and Lindy, millions of us have created our own sisterhood with those who feel closer than our own blood relatives.

Throughout life's trials and triumphs, trusting in each other is the secret to what keeps us women keeping on.

The friend who can be silent with us in a moment of despair or confusion; who can stay with us in an hour of grief and bereavement; who can tolerate not knowing, not curing, not healing; and face us with the reality of our powerlessness. That is the friend who cares.

Henri Nouwen

Cautionary Note:

Sometimes, there are friends you love dearly, yet their *neediness* leaves you exhausted and exasperated. Even with your best intentions to be a true friend, after you've been with them, you feel as if you've been drained by an *emotional leech*. Certainly not a pretty term, however it does describe their effect on your emotional well-being. Is there anyone you consider a friend who requires, expects, and/or demands that you owe them your time, energy, resources or love? If so, think deeply of your intention for this journey. If your friendships feel more like *stress-ships*, would reconsidering those relationships honor your mental and physical health? Trust the signals your intuition sends you. Remember who you are here for. Even more important than finding the love you long for, my hope is that by now your first priority is to protect and nurture *you*.

JOURNEY JOURNALING:

Define *acquaintance*

Define *friend*

Who were my best childhood friends? Why did I choose them?

Who are my best friends now? Why have I chosen them?

What are my personal issues around trusting women?

What does a friend have to do to lose my friendship?

MIRROR MAGIC: *I love you.*

RECOMMENDED READS:

The Fabric of Friendship: Celebrating the Joys, Mending the Tears in Women's Relationships by Joy Carol

The Friends We Keep: A Woman's Quest for the Soul of Friendship by Sarah Zacarias Davis

(Research source: Taylor, S. E., Klein, L.C., Lewis, B. P., Gruenewald, T. L., Gurung, R.A.R., & Updegraff, J. (2000). "Female Responses to Stress: Tend and Befriend, Not Fight or Flight," *Psychological Review*, 107(3), 41-429

9 *Tassels:*
The POWER of Alphabet Soup ~
It's Academic, Girlfriend

When we escaped from Cuba,
all we could carry was our education.
Alicia Coro

Give a girl an education and introduce her properly into the
world, and ten to one but she has the means of settling well,
without further expense to anybody.
Jane Austen

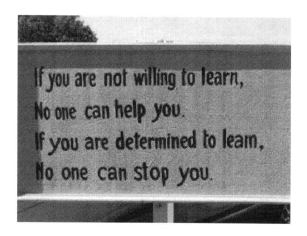

Our Terms:

EDUCATION: The act or process of imparting or acquiring
knowledge; developing the power of reasoning and judgment.

POWER: Great or marked ability to do or act; capability of doing
or accomplishing something; strength; might; force; the possession
of control or command; authority.

MARY

Raised in the traditional home of pre-Betty Friedan's *Feminine Mystique* days, when sons were sent to college for careers, and daughters were sent to the same place for a different reason, the only goal of Mary and her parents for pursuing higher education was for her to earn her MRS. Degree. Even though her father served on the County Board of Education and founded the college their darling daughter now attended, Mary's parents were satisfied with her C average. She happily wasted their tuition on her enthusiastic investment of running on the *bimbo* track (read: Cheerleading major). It was no secret to anyone on campus that she was there for just one reason ~ in hot pursuit of landing her future groom, whoever he may be. Her parents trusted that, sooner or later, she was bound to find the perfect young aspiring graduate who would offer a lifetime of wedded bliss, (Read: financial security for their bimbo daughter).

Had Mary known then what she had to painfully learn later, she would have dedicated more of her youthful energies to acquiring as many of those silly little letters behind her name as she did dates with *cool* seniors.

As fate would have it, in her junior year Mary's friendship with Tom, the senior lead cheerleader, suddenly bloomed into a romance made in heaven, or at least that's what it seemed to her. After their whirlwind romance ~ lasting all of four months ~ Tom got down on one knee and proposed. The very next day Mary's mom rushed her down to the stationers to order the wedding invitations. Evidently, if it was in print he couldn't back out.

Tom had the All-American good looks with the personality to match. He could charm his way in or out of almost any situation, with the exception of his grades, which unfortunately hovered around a 2.8 GPA. His parents warned him that engineering was a very competitive field, and he'd need a Master's Degree to land a job with a major company. It all fell on deaf ears. In the meantime, Mary's meager interest in attending class, much less keeping up her C's, dropped to last place on her priority list. After all, she had the perfectly stunning summer wedding to plan.

Summer quickly arrived. The late afternoon ceremony was the perfect setting to begin their lives together. Two hundred of their closest friends and family smiled perfect smiles, drank perfect champagne, ate the perfect five course gourmet dinner, and wished the newlyweds well on their perfect honeymoon. There was one tiny disappointment to the celebration. Both sets of parents had hoped to announce at the reception where the newlyweds would be moving for graduate school, but Tom's transcripts had fallen short. Every other detail could not have been more perfect for Mary's wedding day.

Tom landed a job as an apprentice at an electrical company, and Mary was hired as a teaching assistant. Her job lasted just as long as it took her to become pregnant, because once the *nesting* instinct kicked in, her only interest was preparing for their perfect child. Tom soon noticed that he'd slipped to second place in Mary's heart because the mommy-to-be was now consumed with decorating the nursery, attending baby showers, reading *baby books,* and preparing for the birth. But, as baby's will do, once Tom saw that adorable face of his newborn son he started dreaming of tossing the ball and going camping with this precious little boy who had stolen his heart.

As planned, Casey grew into a perfect and healthy one-year-old. But at his birthday checkup the pediatrician asked uncomfortable questions that brought Mary out of the denial she'd been afraid to face from almost the beginning. Little Casey avoided eye contact. He didn't mimic sounds or smile when they smiled at him. They had tried to engage him with toys, songs, and peek-a-boo games, but Casey only fixated on the tick tock of the antique clock in the kitchen. After three months of intense testing, Casey was diagnosed with autism. By some odd coincidence, that same day Tom, the perfect husband and father, left Mary and Casey, the perfect wife and child, behind. Their divorce and bankruptcy hearings happened in the same courtroom just two weeks apart.

Mary's second husband, Jack, was a successful corporate attorney with no children and money to burn. Mary saw him as the man who could provide her and her child with the life style she'd hoped to have had with Tom. Reality hit within weeks after their wedding when Jack confronted Mary with a take it or leave it option. Casey was more than his luxury life style could handle. He offered Mary the money to put Casey in a *special* home so that they could travel the world on their own. What he didn't understand was that Casey was her world. A year went by while the three of them lived under Tom's roof, but his put downs to Casey became more and more toxic. Behind his back, Mary found a job and an apartment so that she and her son could start again… again.

Two divorces, and twelve years of working low-paying jobs to raise Casey on her own, Mary began her education in earnest. When Casey wasn't in school, she shared day care with another single mom. She had to work part-time, but with some legitimate credits from her cheerleading days, Mary managed to earn her bachelor's degree in three furious and empowering years.

> *The feminine mystique has succeeded in burying millions of American women alive.*
> Betty Friedan

Imagine ending up dependent on a man you wouldn't have chosen for any other reason than to have a roof over your head and food in your fridge. That's the tragic scenario for so many women with significant economic and educational limitations. They are far more likely to be vulnerable to a new man with the wrong motives if he appears to be her savior. With or without an education, when a woman relies on a man to relieve her of the burden of self-responsibility, she and her children are vulnerable to the inequity of power as she trades her integrity and security for his paycheck. How would that situation feel every night as you lay next to the man who holds your well-being in the palm of his hand? So many of our sisters endure this reality because they lack the education to change it.

Earning your education empowers you to provide for your own needs and wants, whether in a relationship or not. If you are in a relationship, your education affords you true equity with your partner. Of course, financial equity comes to mind. But, consider, too, that financial equity also positions you as an equitable partner in all major choices, such as where you live, what vacations you take, how many children you have, and how you will spend your retirement. Most importantly, being self-sufficient insures you have an equal voice in the dynamics of your relationship.

JAYNE

As more and more women are choosing to pursue education, services have expanded to meet their needs. That was true for Jayne, a 48 year old recently divorced woman, who welcomed the opportunity for the camaraderie of meeting women on the same journey. She was also, understandably, intimidated by the thought of pursuing higher education after two decades of being a wife, mother, and secretary for her husband's business. She was even more intimidated when she learned that returning students, in certain circles, are affectionately known as *retreads* (listed as *non-traditional student* in some college catalogues).

To support the more mature student, many colleges offer counseling for exploring career options that match your personality and areas of strength. Jayne learned of this option when she was confused about choosing her major. Her program counselor made the appointment with the Career Counseling Office to discuss her career history, and have her take a personality assessment.

As the counselor shared the assessment results, she noticed a surprised expression come over Jayne's face. There it was, near the top of her assessment results. Jayne's top two strengths for her personality type: Empathy and Business Organization. So far, so good. That was, however, followed by the #1 recommendation on her career list: Funeral Home Director!

Sensing her shock, the counselor explained, *Funeral Directors do not work with the dead. They comfort the grieving, and offer guidance to make financial decisions about funeral arrangements and payment options. Your empathy and business skills indicate success in following this, or a related, career path.* Jayne did not follow that particular path, choosing instead to become a teacher, but she still smiles thinking that she probably would have been successful owning a mortuary!

Returning to school can feel daunting, especially if, like Jayne, you have been away from education for a while. As one who has been there, trust me, you have nothing to lose, and so much to gain by returning. Not just earning a degree, but you will be exposed to higher learning, and that holds the potential to open your mind and your heart to discover so much new information that you will find interesting, and maybe even fascinating! The classroom discussions and debates generate critical thinking skills that apply to all aspects of your life. And, oh the friends you will make and the experiences you will share!

Scholarships for the Sisterhood

Money is an issue for almost everyone going back to school. The good news is that returning to college after years, maybe decades, often benefits your application for scholarships. Google the *Free Scholarship Search* section or *Scholarships for Nontraditional Students, Distance Learners and Adults Returning to College.* These sites offer comprehensive resources for searching specific scholarships offered with either no age requirements, or scholarships funding non-traditional students.

Colleges and universities provide counselors who can answer questions about what financial aid your school offers. Depending on other responsibilities you carry, you may be able to find a part-time job on or off campus. Speaking of those *other responsibilities* ~ also known as LIFE ~ managing your time will become your number one priority as you juggle attending classes, studying, and writing those endless papers. Arrange your daily schedule with a critical eye to open up those windows of time necessary to get you through each day, semester, and eventually to graduation!

If it has been a few years since you walked into a classroom, one of the most important things to remember, and luckily one of the easiest, is surrounding yourself with those *retreads* I mentioned. Not only do they feel your *pain*, they **share** your pain, and maybe perhaps your sheer terror ~ like only a retread sister can. Watch for them in your classes. They're not hard to spot, by the way. They are the women who look like a deer caught in the headlights! You will grow to depend on each other. You will be each other's support group for the anxiety, and *study buddies* for the grades! Everything I wrote about the Sisterhood in Chapter 6 goes 100% here!

Your Degree is the Most Personal Property You Will Ever Own

In divorce, women can and do lose homes, cars, financial security, even visitation with their children. But, **no one** can ever claim those powerful *alphabet soup* letters behind your name. Your degree is yours alone. You earned your education, and it holds the potential to open doors of opportunity, sometimes in ways that you cannot imagine now.

Advantages of earning your education:

- Exercises your brain and builds your mental capacity for learning

- Expands your sisterhood to women who share your commitment to personal growth

- Provides economic freedom and autonomy

- Opens doors to options and opportunities
- Establishes your voice in the world
- Increases your confidence and self-respect
- Gives you ownership of your most personal property
- Empowers you to choose a man for the right reasons

> *Our destinies are the culmination of all the choices we've made along the way, which is why it's imperative to listen hard to your inner voice when it speaks up.*
> *Don't let anyone else's noise drown it out."*
> Megan McCafferty, Second Helpings

One word of warning: Higher education does not ensure that one will not make bimbo choices in one's life. A degree provides knowledge. Wisdom is a whole other thing. What higher education does offer are greater options and opportunities to design the life you want. What your journey provides is your core belief that you deserve it!

JOURNEY JOURNALING:

How does my level of education impact my life choices?

What women do I respect because of their education?

If higher education interests me, what actions do I need to take to attain it?

If higher education interests me, what date will I start the process?

MIRROR MAGIC: *Me, a student? Me, a student!*

10 Cinderella Revisited:
aka "CinderFella" ~ It's ALL About the Slipper

Let me see if it will not fit me.
Cinderella

Our Terms:

FANTASY: Extravagant, unrestrained imagination; imagined, abnormal, or bizarre sequence of events, especially if provoked by unfulfilled psychological need; supposition based on no solid evidence.

FACT: Something that actually exists; reality; a truth known by observation.

FIT: Adapted or suited; appropriate; proper or becoming; qualified or competent.

DESPERATE: Frantic, anxious, hopeless; reckless or dangerous because of despair or urgency; having lost hope; desperate spirit crying for relief.

DISCERN: To perceive, recognize, or distinguish through intellect.

CHRISTINE

Though difficult to admit to herself, Christine was suffering the pains of yet another failed romance. To lend some moral support, the next morning her younger sister Emily dropped by her house. Soon their conversation turned to how their little girl dreams of fairy tale romances had, over and over through their adult years, been dashed to pieces by reality.

Christine's daughter, Caroline, was now grown-up and on her own, but they both remembered her mother's solemn vow that her daughter's world would be free from all the nonsense of fairy tales. That lasted until her fourth birthday when Caroline insisted on a Princess theme ~ or else she was calling Grandma! Two decades later, Caroline's master's thesis debated the merits of *Pretty Woman in the Post-Feminist Era.*

For many women, our little girl fantasies come alive with the romantic story of *Cinderella,* still considered to be one of the world's most beloved fairy tales. Its theme of poor girl makes good has been retold in countless variations across time, cultures and mediums, including opera, ballet, film, books, novels, television, musical theater, even video games, and performed in at least thirty languages, from Afrikaans to Ukrainian.

What is it about this fantastical tale that continues to hold such power to mesmerize little girls over centuries of retelling? Could it be that *Cinderella* holds some hidden wisdom, some juicy secret to guide us into womanhood? Was there a purpose when the weaver of *Cinderella* chose a glass slipper as the bait to lure her true love to her door? Couldn't she just as easily have dropped her glove, her cape or her tiara as she ran panic-stricken against the stroke of midnight?

The man who penned our current *Cinderella,* Charles Perrault, a 17th century French attorney, could obviously not have compared notes with the tale's original author, Strabo from 1st century BCE, so it's hard to say if either or both of them understood the significance of footwear to women. Nevertheless, Strabo's *Cinderella* introduced a handmaiden's flying sandal landing on the unsuspecting head of a king as the original story idea. Seventeen hundred years later, Mr. Perrault morphed that sandal into our beloved glass slipper. Granted, this was a very long time to keep one storyline alive and well. Even more fascinating is that regardless of all of the varying styles of footwear woven over the years into this enchanting tale, every male author had enough understanding of the female situation to use shoes as the way to win the heart of a prince!

But before we get to the reason for the all-important slipper, we need to address Mr. Perrault's original version, which was a bit dicier than the sanitized tale we grew up with. This first *Cinderella* story shines a very bright light on the dark side of a woman's desperation, as in when Prince Charming's party of yore showed up at their cottage, the wicked stepsisters, so desperate to marry royalty, were willing to give up their personal power, plus a body part or two, to wed him. The story goes that when the Prince saw the blood streaming from the stepsister's shoe... *It was then he knew this was not his true bride.*

Perrault deliciously sets up the scene with those nasty stepsisters, Drusilla and Anastasia, caught in their obscene desperation to try and fool not an everyday, run-of-the-mill prince, but a real **Prince Charming**. In their first attempt to prove the shoe would fit, they were willing to excuse themselves just long enough to pinch and stuff their little tootsies into that glorious glass slipper. Ah, but as he tried to slip the slipper onto each foot, the task proved utterly impossible. So, not giving up easily, they excused themselves a second time for just long enough to grab a butcher's knife from the kitchen to cut off those very same *slightly too large for a royal slipper* tootsies. Evidently some women will do anything to grab them a prince.

Plastic Surgery for Fitting Feet in High Heels is Still Happening. Still Probably Not a Good Idea
CBS Morning Show, 4/26/2012

But now, back to our question: *How did the male authors of Cinderella know that shoes were eternally a really big deal for women?* We of the sisterhood have walked in shoes, slippers, sandals, yes, even stilettos that are too long, too short, too wide, too narrow, too high, too whatever. We equate this torture to water-boarding. However, ill-fitting gloves, a misshaped velvet cape, or a slightly imperfect tiara? Not so much.

So, given the desperation of the stepsisters to wed a prince at any cost, the moral of this particular version is *How could either have danced through their wedding, much less years of marriage, with a spring in their step or joy in their soul? Wouldn't every time they saw not love, but regret in the eyes of their prince, this would remind them they were, indeed, not loved?* Could that be why shoes are the centerpiece of thousands of years of Cinderella themes ~ because somehow those authors of old somehow intuitively, miraculously knew that *happily ever after* is impossible when a woman sells her soul to dance with a faux prince who offers her ill-fitting shoes?

As the world moved into the modern era, writers have slowly but surely imbued Cinderella with options that empower her to choose the course of her life. The Opera *Irmelin,* written by Frederick Delius in 1892, exchanged the glass slipper and beady-eyed stepsisters for the novel idea of a more self-assured princess. When King Daddy ordered his daughter to marry the prince he chose, she responded, *See 'ya!*

The story tells of the lovely Princess Irmelin, whose hand is sought by suitors, far and wide. As the story opens, Princess Irmelin sits gazing out of the window of her room in the royal castle. Her maid chides her about how she ignores all of the knights eager to have her hand in marriage. But, only Irmelin can hear the voice in the air persuading her that her true love is soon to appear.

Irmelin's father, intent on seeing his daughter wed, introduces her to three suitor knights: the first old, the second fair, the third grasping for royalty. Irmelin turns them all down. None of them interests her in the least because she has her own dreams of the man she will marry, and believes he will soon appear. Even so, she is told by her father that she must marry in six months. Finally, against her will, her father betroths her to a powerful neighboring prince.

Another prince from a distant land, Nils, has been chasing his own dreams by following a river he is sure will lead him to his ideal princess. Back at Irmelin's castle, six months have passed ~ and the betrothal of the unwilling Princess is taking place that same day. When Nils appears at the castle gate, the King does not recognize him as a prince. Instead, he orders him to sing songs of love to the bride as she waits in the castle garden. As Nils enters the garden, there walks Irmelin, weeping over her fate, forever lost to her own dream of love. Upon the sight of her, Nils calls her by name for she is his ideal ~ the realization of his dreams. As day breaks, they are far gone from the castle and King Daddy, as they followed the Silver Stream towards their own dreams of happily ever after.

Which Cinderella Would You Choose to Be?

The following original fairy tale progresses, as your journey has, from desperation to Dignity; from shifting the question *Will he like me?* to *Is he WORTHY of Me?*

The Tale of Two Princesses

Once upon a time there was a princess. From commoners to royalty, everyone agreed her foolishness did not suit one born to the Crown. Poor little *dripping in diamonds and desperation* princess was *oh! so tired* of being alone in her castle that she ordered all the men of her kingdom and beyond to her Royal Ball. In so doing, she would lure all of the princes, far and wide, to view her in her finery. Believing her Prince Charming would surely attend, princess slept like a baby the night before the Ball.

The next evening she arrived wearing a golden gown, designed to catch the eye of her *prince-to-be.* The princess searched every face in the room, but alas, she found him not. So, Plan B put her perfect prince-to-be on the back burner as her inner voice whispered: *Well, if not my perfect prince, then somebody else will have to do.* She danced with every reluctant princely version of Tom, Dick and Harry, plus every other man she could pull onto the floor. Of course, each one in turn stepped and stomped all over her beautiful glass slippers just so they could be excused from her ever tightening arms. Not surprisingly, the evening ended badly with the foolish princess alone in her bed for the rest of her royal life.

Now in the Kingdom across the river, there lived another princess who was respected throughout the land. She ruled her people with great wisdom and compassion. Just as she ruled her people, she ruled herself, as well. She knew that doing what was in her best interest would serve the best interests of her people.

But alas, even though her subjects adored her as their princess, she was lonely for the man who would love her as a woman. She decreed a Royal Ball throughout her Kingdom and beyond. She would find the one who would respect her mind, nurture her dreams, and find in her the deepest longing of his soul. She would not compromise.

Admittance to her Ball required one special object. Each suitor was to design a unique slipper, fit for only her. As the guests entered the Ball, each hopeful offered the princess the slipper he hoped would satisfy her requirements. Throughout the evening she tried on each slipper, but alas not one of them fit, so could not fulfill her heart's desire.

Towards midnight a prince arrived from a kingdom far away. His hand held the required slipper. His heart held the hope that it would please her for he had dreamt of her in a million dreams. He had known everything about her except where she was. Even having never seen her face, his slipper reflected all he knew her to be. When he arrived at the front of the line, he reached for the slipper hidden in his cape. He was not surprised when it easily slipped onto her foot. In true amazement, the princess looked at the slipper and then into his eyes, for what he had created was perfectly *her*. Prepared for the reality he trusted would be his, he revealed the mate, the perfect complement to the first. Through the night they danced with ease. In fact, the slippers fit so perfectly the princess forgot she was wearing them at all!

* * * * * * * * *

Imagine listening to these two fairytales when you were a child. Wouldn't you have cheered for the wise princess, who, with such self-awareness would recognize the slipper, and thus, the prince meant for her? She might not have known the height of the heel, or if it was open or closed toe, but she knew when shoes fit her so perfectly that she could dance like a dream through the night with the prince who valued her beyond all others.

The CinderFELLA Project

By the time Christine and Emily had traveled down the *Memory Lane of Love's Lost* that afternoon, they decided to take their grains of insight and turn the tables on the Cinderella story by designing their own glass slippers to see which prince fit their ideal. Each sister wrote her list of princely qualities that drew her to the men she had loved, starting with fathers, brothers, uncles, ex-husbands, friends and lovers.

What were the qualities of these men that attracted them? What qualities were the deal breakers, or screamed *Red Flag, Red Flag*? Eventually one column expanded to three as their lists prioritized the most to least important items. With their permission, here are the features of their CinderFella slippers.

Christine's List:

Priority	Would Be Nice	Yeah Right!
Integrity	Great hair	Ballroom dancer
Intelligence	Tall	Grown children
Sense of humor	Broad chest	Appreciates poetry
Health conscious	Business owner	Owns a winery
Gracious	History buff	Mercedes SL
Handsome widower	Enjoys traveling	Loves opera

Emily's List:

Priority	Would Be Nice	Yeah Right!
Compassionate	Antique lover	Dog breeder
Intelligent	Ballroom dancer	Plays the cello
Quick wit	Back-road cyclist	Enjoys the sunrise
Health conscious	Scuba diver	Has grown children
Optimist	Owns large home	Cottage on the coast
Travels	College degree	Graduate degree
Loves animals	Loves independent bookstores	Gives good massage

Once they knew the details of their *slippers*, Christine and Emily could each look for the man with the qualities that would complete her, to bring her heart *home*. They were no longer looking for a special someone, but for THE One.

When you are choosing who will fill your eyes every morning across your breakfast table, and who you will invite into your bed, your body, your soul, and your future ~ with all that it may bring ~ would it not serve you to know the size of your custom, one-of-a-kind, CinderFella slippers that please only you? Would it not serve you to take all the time you need to know everything you need to know about the Prince you seek? That is, if you want that dance to begin as soon as possible, dancing soul-to-soul forever, with a smile on your face and joy in your heart.

A Cautionary Note:

When a woman claims her power to choose for herself the man who would be her *Prince*, there can appear those who may feel threatened (such as those pesky controllers), as they will likely not appreciate her self-determination. Always eager to give advice, they are happy to warn you: *You're just too particular!* or *Give him a chance. Nobody's perfect,* or *Aren't you setting your sites just a bit too high?* or *He's nice/wealthy/tall/short/has nice teeth/is a great dancer/has a great personality.* They go on... *He's perfect for you,* and *He really, really, really wants to date you!* You know how to respond to those who try to push your feet into shoes that don't fit. You also know when you have found your perfect match ~ whether searching for shoes or a glass slipper ~ when you, not they, hold your perfect mate!

JOURNEY JOURNALING:

Who are my memorable men and why?

What were my feelings when describing my slipper?

What have I lost of myself in my search for love?

How have I tried to hide the bleeding?

How will my search be different now?

MIRROR MAGIC: *I will know.*

I'm not a happy-ending person. I want to know what happens once Cinderella rides off with Prince Charming.

Melissa Joan Hart

* * * * *

Cinderella's Diary

I miss my stepmother. What a thing to say but it's true. The prince is so boring: four hours to dress and then the cheering throngs. Again. The page that holds the door is cute enough to eat. Where is he once Mr. Charming kisses my forehead goodnight?

Every morning I gaze out a casement window at the hunters, dark men with blood on their boots who joke and mount, their black trousers straining, rough beards, callused hands, selfish, abrupt...

Oh, dear diary ~I am lost in ever after: Those insufferable birds, someone in every room with a lute, the queen calling me to look at another painting of her son, this time holding the transparent slipper I wish I'd never seen.

(Permission to reprint granted by Red Hen Press)

11 *Mirror, Mirror On The Wall,*
He Might First See You at the Mall

If I do not believe myself worth wooing,
I am surely not worth winning.
H.L. Longfellow

You must have been a beautiful baby
'cuz Baby, look at you now!
Johnny Mercer

Our Terms:

DIGNITY: Manner indicative of self-respect; manner of nobility or elevation of character; worthiness and respect.

SELF-RESPECT: Proper esteem or regard for the dignity of one's character.

WORTHY: Having adequate or great merit, character, or value; commendable, excellence, deserving.

ILLUMINE: Brighten; light up; glow, gleam, shine; sparkle.

CONGRUENT: Agreeable; harmonious.

LISA

Lisa had been skinny all her life. Some would say too skinny. Whenever friends commented about her weight, Lisa explained that her appearance was important to her, and that she felt more in control if she looked as perfect as she could. For Lisa, being in control meant not taking risks, so she dressed her anorexia, both day and night, in gray, beige or black.

Even though Lisa tried to look and be perfect, her love life was anything but. As proof, she had suffered through several less than perfect relationships. Determined her love life must be as perfect as the rest of her life, she made an appointment with a therapist that her best friend had recommended.

As the sessions progressed, Lisa began exploring memories and feelings about her father, who had died ten years before. During one especially intense session, the therapist had Lisa sit facing an empty chair and visualize her father sitting there. Then, with no fear of reprisal, she was to tell him every feeling that she still felt for him.

Lisa stared at that empty chair for quite a while. The cold, dense metal seemed to stare back at her, almost as if the chair was daring her to utter even a single whisper. Finally, after what seemed like hours, she tried to speak. As her lips struggled to form the words, she felt as if someone had their hands around her throat. Terrified, tears began to fall on her cheeks just seconds before she felt overwhelmed with what could only be described as an emotional tsunami. Through her uncontrollable sobbing, she tried again to speak, choking on each precious word. Conflicting emotions were warring within her ~ wanting to stay silent to stay safe; wanting to let every word fly. Finally, like flood waters bursting through a breach, Lisa released her scream.

The lifelong silence of her little girl's shattered heart exploded into a woman's rage! Control-obsessed Lisa was now beyond noticing her loss of control. She forgot about the therapist. She forgot about how she looked, or how she sounded. She forgot about the chair. The release of her father's violation was uncontrollable, unstoppable. Then, as her soul broke free from his chains, her intuition brought forward something unfamiliar ~ for the first time in her life she felt flushed with power! What would take some time for her to realize was that her butterfly wings had just pushed through the confines of her childhood cocoon, and those gorgeous wings were already unfolding in readiness for flight. Her therapist knew Lisa's breakdown was in reality the breakthrough that would trade her desperation to be perfect in the tormented eyes of her father for her freedom to be herself.

On the way home, Lisa stopped to buy her first-ever quart of Haagen-Dazs. Before her next session she had gained five pounds and begun to glow. Over the next few days she reconnected with women to whom she hadn't been such a good friend. Thankfully, those bridges had not been burned. They welcomed her back into the circle, because beneath Lisa's *control freak* persona they'd always known how wonderful she really was.

I read and walked for miles at night along the beach, writing bad blank verse and searching endlessly for someone wonderful who would step out of the darkness and change my life. It never crossed my mind that that person could be me.

Anna Quindlen

The following six months brought powerful changes to Lisa's way of being in this world. She learned to say *No!* to *I should be perfect.* Her happy heart now high-fived every *What am I pretending not to know,* and shushed every *should.* She no longer got sucked into the drama that had controlled her life before her breakthrough. Rather, she noticed the drama on the stage of her life from the comfort of her cushy seat high above in the balcony as she sat sipping champagne with Statler and Waldorf.

She also noticed that her rather *uptight and boring* wardrobe didn't feel right anymore, as in *uptight and boring.* So, soon after her Haagen-Dazs baptism, Goodwill was busy hanging her *skinny* clothes on their racks while her closet and hips started filling out a bit. As Lisa's journey was now unraveling the chrysalis bonds of her life to finally set her free to fly, she made another discovery that every butterfly worthy of her wings knows, but moths will never understand. Clothes come in colors! So does jewelry, scarves, hats and SHOES! And in those new shoes Lisa was standing straight and walking tall ~ the better to look people in the eye. Now she said what she meant, sometimes even with new found grace. She had become as true on the outside as she was on the inside.

Yes, Lisa had definitely traded in *emaciated* for **Amazing!** And, no surprise ~ the more she loved herself, the more men started noticing. Some even asked her out. Ah, but Lisa trusted her tummy. Both her intuition and her intelligence rang in loud and clear: *Girlfriend, you need a little more time to fall in love with yourself before you're primed to find your Prince.* And being wise, she took her own advice. Although she never had a session quite as intense as her breakthrough episode, Lisa continued with her therapist on a healing journey very similar to the one you've traveled on through these pages.

Like you, Lisa promised to:

- Be who I am, which happens to be *wonderful!*
- Expect respect from others
- Never ever allow myself to be used or abused
- Never ever settle for less than what I deserve
- Trust my tummy
- Ask for what I want and need from others
- Make choices true to my core values
- Choose what I want, not what others want for me
- Dress as though I was a gift
- Be my own *Gentle Observer*
- Give my brilliance to the light rather than the darkness

Confidence is Your Ultimate Beauty Secret

Your journey has birthed the power for an authentic shift. You have cleared away all the cobwebs and brick walls that held you back from the life and love you deserve. You know you are worthy of the prince of your choosing, if you so choose. Now, it's the world's turn to know what you know ~ that you are an extraordinary, radiant woman.

1st Impressions Last Forever

It's human instinct to first *size up* a person visually. Biologically, it is a survival skill that has kept homo sapiens alert and alive for millions of years. However, in the 21st century we can safely say we've taken the visual alert to a whole new level. Even just standing in the checkout line, our eyes rivet to the best-selling magazines ~ with covers dripping with air-brushed models and celebrities with perfect hair, perfect teeth, and perfect bodies wearing perfect clothes. Our compulsion to *look* proves that marketing professionals rely on how consumed with the physical we have become.

No surprise, the same thing happens when YOU walk into someone's view. Within seconds, people note your appearance and you note theirs. By the way we dress, move and speak, each of us gives the viewer certain impressions about what sort of person we are. There's even research to prove it.

You Never Get a 2nd Chance to Make a 1st Impression

The *HALO EFFECT* ~ named by researcher, Dr. Edward Thorndike ~ describes an innate cognitive bias that colors our judgments of a person's character by our overall first impression. According to this research, when your presence projects a positive visual image, others assume that everything about you and your life is positive. The opposite is just as true.

Something in the Way She Moves Attracts Me
Like No Other Lover
George Harrison

As you enter a room, even if you're shaking inside (and we all are at one time or another), when you walk tall, when you look people in the eye as you shake their hands, when you look as great on the outside as you feel on the inside, you give an impression of a woman who knows and loves what she's about. And a woman that projects self-confidence attracts others who agree with her. In other words, taking your appearance seriously can transform your life.

I never go out unless I look like Joan Crawford, the movie star.
If you want to see the girl next door, go next door.
Joan Crawford

When we talk about *looking the part*, it's not because you are on the hunt for a prince, but because you are ~ first and foremost ~ a unique and amazing woman. Before your journey takes you across the threshold of your private world into the world beyond your front door, you may appreciate some guidance to go forth in confidence, being the best you can be. And, now that you live in reality rather than as *Denial Diva*, let's get the *elephant in the room* right up here, front and center.

Weight: There it is ~ specifically, your weight. No way to deny it. From anorexic to obese, body weight is what we can't help noticing first. And, be honest, it is your own weight that comes into awareness first thing in the morning, last thing at night, and pretty much all through the day. Every time you see your reflection in a mirror, or stare in disbelief at the cover model on COSMO, when you struggle to climb a few stairs or exchange size eight for a ten, maybe twelve, maybe more ~ there it is, and so is the state of your health. You'd have to be living in a cave to not know that your weight becomes the primary concern of your doctor if pounds become too few or too many. The term *ideal weight* means just that! *Ideal*, as in healthiest.

I drive way too fast to worry about cholesterol.
Author Unknown

In today's world you can't turn the corner or surf the net without another expert discussing how important diet and exercise are to maximize your physical and mental well-being. As you are reading this book to create love in your life, how many times did creating the body you love cross your mind? If your physical well-being hasn't crossed your mind by now ~ as in being as healthy as you can possibly be ~ it might be time to go back a few chapters and re-read... just sayin'...

> ***When it comes to eating right and exercising, there is no 'I'll start tomorrow.' Tomorrow is a disease.***
> Terri Guillemets

As a breast cancer survivor and Wellness Coach, the following are my primary recommendations for my clients:

- Eat foods that feed health and fight disease

- Research and address your specific risk factors

- Blood and muscles require oxygen, so... to keep your body and brain happy and healthy... exercise!

- Find medical professionals that emphasize health and disease prevention

- Stress puts your physical and mental health at risk, so surround yourself with people who have earned your trust and bring you joy

- Nurture, nurture, nurture you

(Please seek advice from your healthcare professional before following any of the above suggestions.)

> ***Half the modern drugs could be thrown out the window, except that the birds might eat them.***
> M. H. Fischer

Dress shabbily and they remember the dress.
Dress impeccably and they remember the woman.
Coco Chanel

As Cinderella's fairy godmother knew, presentation is everything. Let's face it, before *What Not to Wear* was cancelled, a lot of us were addicted! We relished watching each *Plain Jane*, with her closet-from-hell, learn to choose the right clothes, makeup, and hair style that transformed her into a real beauty! Ever notice that by the end of the show looking great gave her confidence? And all in less than an hour? Amazing!

But what if this new self-confident charmer was looking for your Prince Charming? Well, in that case, this might be the perfect time to check in with your *Mirror, Mirror on the Wall* to see how you fare with all the growing competition!

I don't understand how a woman can leave the house without
fixing herself up a little, if only out of politeness.
And then, you never know, maybe that's the day she has a date
with destiny. And it's best to be as pretty as possible for destiny.
Coco Channel

You know, Cinderella had it easy. With the wave of a wand, and a bit of *Bibbity Bobbity Boo,* her fairy godmother morphed her from rags to riches, then sent her off to the Ball looking like the Princess she was about to become. In the real world this all gets a bit more complicated. Chances are your prince will first see you dressed for the mall, not the Ball. Plus, your chances of being the next TV makeover are slim. You could hire a fashion savvy godmother, as in *fashion consultant*, but if $$$ is beyond your budget, what are you to do when the whole point is to leave a first impression that leaves a potential prince wanting more?

The Do It Yourself Makeover

The following pages provide guidance about how to choose makeup, colors, even jewelry to compliment your coloring. And, because your face is where the magic really happens, that's where we'll start… with your face. Of course, if you're thinking, *How 'bout I start with something else?* remember Cindy Crawford's immortal words: *Even I don't wake up looking like Cindy Crawford.* Your face is your focus, specifically the colors of your face. Using the power of color to compliment your eyes, skin, and hair will make magic happen! Your eyes will sparkle and your complexion will glow!

On the other hand, glowing is practically impossible when you wear colors that clash with your own. For example, if you have watercolor eyes, translucent skin, and hair the color of soft wheat, imagine the catastrophe of deep bronze makeup, double black eyeliner, and a day glow dress with dark chunky jewelry. Right! Not good! The strong colors overpower your own, and POOF! **You** disappear.

If your skin tone is deep and warm, wearing colors paler than your own can wash out the richness of your natural glow. The result can be the dreaded effect of making your eyes look tired and your skin look dull. Again, not good, as *glowing* is definitely a plus for first impressions, especially when your prince will remember forever the first time he saw your face. So, in the hopes of remedying such horror, on the following pages you'll find the *Must Knows* to help you **Go for the Glow**!

Understanding Basic Color Analysis

Many fashion consultants and plastic surgeons rely on the International Munsell Color System to accurately determine a client's color palette. This scientific system is based on three components: Hue, Value, and Chroma.

Hue is simply the color's name. Simple Hues: Red, Yellow, Green, Blue and Purple. Compound hues: Yellow-Red, Green-Yellow, Blue-Green, Purple-Blue and Red-Purple.

Value: How light or dark a color is. The more white in a color, the higher the value. True black has the lowest value; true white has the highest value.

Chroma: The clarity or strength of the color. Muted, grayed colors have low chroma; clear, vibrant, bright colors have high chroma.

How to Determine Your Makeup Colors

Foundation: Match your skin tone at the outer corner of your eyes. Blend the makeup on your face and neck, and then match to your skin tone in both indoor lighting and sunlight. Hint: To ensure you choose the correct foundation color, take a friend along for a second opinion.

The tricky part is determining if your skin tone is *cool* or *warm*. This applies to all skin tones from fair to dark and all ethnicities from Asian to Caucasian to African-American to Hispanic. Regardless of race, your skin has undertones that tend either *cool* or *warm*.

Eye Color: Use your brow color for mascara, eye liner and brow pencil. For more drama, increase the color value. Choose shadow in your eye or brow color. Hint: Your eyes contain a rainbow of colors. Use a magnifying mirror to see the full spectrum.

Lipstick and Blush: Match to your cheeks and lips. Gently pinch both cheeks and lips, noting if the color goes pink, red, or orange.

With a bit of practice your makeup routine will take you from ordinary to glowing in five minutes or less.

How to Determine Your Wardrobe Colors

Many of us believe we can't wear certain colors. The truth is that all colors are on a spectrum of Hue, Value and Chroma. Understanding, for example, that the full spectrum for *red* ranges from yellow-red to purple-red, from pastel pink to deepest burgundy, opens up your choices to find the reds that compliment your coloring.

Reds: Your cheek and lip colors.

Greens & Blues: Determined from your eye color. To determine what colors these are, use a magnifying mirror. You will be amazed at the rainbow of colors within your iris. For brown or black eyes, use a color wheel to match your eye color to complimentary greens or blues. www.realcolorwheel.com/colorwheel.htm.

Yellows: Trickiest of all colors to determine. Usually Summers and Springs wear soft, pale yellow; Falls wear golden yellow; Winters wear intense, bright yellow.

Neutrals: Determined by current or former (if your hair is colored or grayed) natural hair color, and eyes if primarily brown or black. Use neutrals for suits, coats, skirts, pants, jackets, shoes and purses to build the core of your wardrobe.

Basic Style Descriptions:

Color analysts often use the four seasons to harmonize skin, eye and hair color with the complimentary fashion style. To define each style, the promotional images of the four celebrities below represent examples of the four styles. About fifty percent of us also have a secondary season. If a celebrity's photo exhibits a secondary, it is noted in parenthesis.

SUMMER: The Look of Yesterday ~ Cool undertones

Actress Cate Blanchett is a *Summer*

FASHION STYLE: Soft, subtle, elegant, delicate, romantic, serene, nostalgic, blended tone on tone, minimal contrast.

COMPLEXION: Clear, cool, delicate.

HAIR COLOR: Ash blonde, light to medium cool red or brown; matures to salt and pepper, cool or icy white.

EYE COLOR: Iris ~ Soft green, blue, hazel, amber or cool brown; Sclera (white surrounding the iris) ~ Gray or white.

COLORS: Minimal to moderate intensity, soft, grayed, translucent, water color tones.

NEUTRALS: Cool tones of tan, beige, soft white, cool gray.

JEWELRY: Silver, white gold, pearls, crystals.

BRIDAL GOWN: Cool white, silver.

AVOID: Contrast, dark colors, earth tones, gold accessories.

Celebs: Charlize Theron (Spring secondary), Cate Blanchett, Meryl Streep, Nicole Kidman, Grace Kelly, Sarah Jessica Parker (Spring secondary), Scarlett Johansson (Spring secondary), Jennifer Love Hewitt, Judy Dench, Diane Sawyer.

FALL: The Look of Nature ~ Warm golden undertones

Actress Halle Berry is a *Fall*

FASHION STYLE: Earthy, warm, fiery, golden, exotic, sensual.

COMPLEXION: Warm tones of olive or gold, may have freckles or appear mottled.

HAIR COLOR: Warm gold, brown, red, chestnut, auburn; matures to warm white, salt and pepper.

EYE COLOR: Iris – Warm gold, green, hazel, amber, brown; Sclera – Warm off-white.

COLORS: Warm, golden colors across the color spectrum.

NEUTRALS: Warm browns, tans, beiges, forest greens, khaki, rust.

JEWELRY: Gold, copper, tortoise shell, semi-precious stones, feathers, wood, shells.

BRIDAL GOWN: Warm off-white, beige, champagne.

AVOID: Black, black with white, grey, pastels, clear chroma.

Celebs: Celebs: Angelina Jolie, Jennifer Lopez, Cindy Crawford (winter secondary), Oprah Winfrey, Julia Roberts (Summer secondary), Halle Berry, Salma Hayek, Julianne Moore, Sophia Loren,, Queen Latifah (Spring secondary), Barbra Streisand.

WINTER: The Look of Sophistication ~ Cool undertones

Actress Isabella Rosselini is a *Winter*

FASHION STYLE: Sophisticated, sleek, high contrast, dramatic, expensive, powerful, uncluttered, modern, angled, vivid.

COMPLEXION: Pearlized, clear, cool, translucent.

HAIR COLOR: Black, ebony, dark cool brown; matures to silvery or icy white.

Note: Lightening or highlighting hair diminishes the *power* of Winter's contrast.

EYE COLOR: Iris: Black or very dark; Sclera Pure

COLORS: Icy, high intensity, bright, jewel tones, clear and cool.
Note: Only Winters wear black, or black and white as colors.

NEUTRALS: Black, cool gray, pure white.

JEWELRY: Silver, white gold, gem stones, rhinestones.

BRIDAL GOWN: Icy white.

AVOID: Earth tones, pastels, fluff!!

Celebs: Snow White, Catherine Zeta Jones (Fall secondary), Elizabeth Taylor (Summer secondary), Lisa Minelli, Marlo Thomas, Eva Longoria, Lucy Liu, Isabella Rossellini

SPRING: The Look of Today ~ Warm undertones

Actress Jennifer Aniston is a *Spring*

FASHION STYLE: Crisp, modern, bright, sunny, curvy, energetic, youthful.

COMPLEXION: Clear, moderately warm to moderately cool.

HAIR COLOR: Golden, strawberry or ash blonde, auburn, red, light to dark warm brown; matures to salt and pepper, warm gray or white.

EYE COLOR: Iris – Green, blue, hazel, brown, amber;

COLORS: Clear, warm, bright.

NEUTRALS: Warm white, beige, tan, brown, navy, soft black.

JEWELRY: Gold, silver, semi-precious stones, plastic.

BRIDAL GOWN: Off-white to cream.

AVOID: Muted or high intensity colors.

Celebs: Reese Witherspoon, Rene Zellweger (Summer secondary), Cameron Diaz, Rachel Ray (Fall secondary), Jennifer Aniston, Reba McEntire (Fall secondary), Ellen DeGeneres, Jada Pinkett Smith (Fall secondary), Meg Ryan, Katie Holmes (Winter secondary), Kirsten Dunst (Summer secondary), Dakota Fanning (Summer secondary), Debra Messing (Fall secondary), Diane Keaton (Summer secondary).

These descriptions only touch the surface of how color transforms your self-image to help you create unforgettable first impressions. The services of a professional consultant, preferably one trained in the Munsell System, are invaluable for assessing your color palette, complimentary prints, accessories, makeup, body proportion, and both your fashion and hair style.

Fees can range from $200 to $1000+, but, considering the money you've wasted buying makeup that just never worked, and clothes still hanging with their price tags in the back of your closet as you cry *I have nothing to wear!,* a professional analysis can be a bargain. In the meantime, here's a list of shopping hints to help get your transformation started.

Shopping Hints

1. To build a coordinated wardrobe list your lifestyle options, such as professional, casual, evening, and athletic clothing. For each option, purchase a core outfit, such as a professional suit, a cocktail dress, slacks and complimentary jacket, plus a few blouses, sweaters, and workout clothes.

2. You don't need a king's ransom to look like a million dollars. Even drug stores carry quality makeup. For quality clothes and accessories, shop End of Season sales, or consignment and thrift stores. Gather your *other seasons* sisters for a wardrobe swap meet. Some of my favorite clothes, scarves, and jewelry have come from just such an event!

3. Collect color swatches by asking a fabric store or seamstress to save you fabric scraps in your color palette. Also, don't forget your closet. If you already own colors in your palette (Hint: these are the colors that when you wear them, you get compliments!), cut a small swatch from inside the hem and keep in an envelope to bring when you shop.

4. If you spy something great, first match the item to your colors. Next, hold the item by your face, then ask the Million $ question:

Does this color compliment or clash with my natural coloring? If the color compliments your skin, try it on to check that the fit flatters your body. If color and fit are both a *yes,* the price is right, and you love it, for goodness sakes **buy it!** If color and fit are a *no,* no matter how much you love it, pass. Remember, you glow when the colors that you wear compliment rather than compete with the colors that you are.

5.   To spice up any outfit, think accessories. Items like scarves, jewelry, hats, vests, purses, and sunglasses can be a thrifty girl's best friends! How important can accessories be? Well, before you run out to the mall in those great fitting jeans, take one minute to add sunglasses and earrings, or throw a beautiful scarf around the collar of your coat. In exchange for that little bit of time, you will radiate *I care how I look, and I look and feel great!* Not a bad first vibe, especially for an unsuspecting prince watching extraordinary you emerge from an ordinary crowd of harried shoppers.

> **Love yourself first and everything else falls in line. You really have to love yourself to get anything done in this world.**
> Lucille Ball

JOURNEY JOURNALING:

How do I feel about creating a public persona that reflects who I am on the inside?

What 3 fashion and 3 make up changes would improve my self-confidence?

What 3 women impress me most with their personal style? Why?

MIRROR MAGIC: *Hello Gorgeous!*

RECOMMENDED READS:

The Body Type Diet and Lifetime Nutrition Plan by Dr. Abravanel, Elizabeth King Morrison

RECOMMENDED READS:

The Body Type Diet and Lifetime Nutrition Plan by Dr. Abravanel, Elizabeth King Morrison

Eat Right for Your Type: The Individualized Diet Solution to Staying Healthy, Living Longer and Achieving Your Ideal Weight by Dr. Peter D'Adamo, Catherine Whitney

12 *On A Clear Day You Can See Who You Are*

*Being powerful is like being a lady. If you have to
tell people you are, you aren't.*
Margaret Thatcher

Just go out there and do what you have to do.
Martina Navratilova

*Don't be afraid your life will end.
Be afraid that it will never begin.*
Grace Hansen

Our Terms:

CLEAR: Free from darkness, obscurity, or cloudiness; transparent, easily seen; sharply defined.

CONFIDENCE: Full trust; belief in the powers, trustworthiness, or reliability of a person or thing: belief in oneself and one's abilities; self-confidence; self-reliance; having no uncertainty about one's own abilities, correctness, success.

STRONG: Power or force: especially able, competent, or powerful, of great moral power, firmness, or courage: strong under temptation.

COMPLETE: Having all parts or elements; whole; entire; full: finished; ended; concluded; perfect in kind or quality; thorough; total; undivided, uncompromised, or unmodified: a complete victory; to make whole; to make perfect; to bring to an end; to finish.

SHINE: To give forth or glow with light; shed or cast light; to be bright with reflected light; glisten; sparkle; to be or appear unusually animated or bright; to appear with brightness or clearness.

CELEBRATION: To rejoice in or have special festivities to mark a happy day, event; to praise publicly; proclaim.

SAGE: A profoundly wise person; venerated for the possession of judgment and experience; marked by calm intuitive judgment.

The beauty of a woman is not in the clothes she wears,
the figure that she carries, or the way she combs her hair.
The beauty of a woman is seen in her eyes, because that is
the doorway to her heart, the place where love resides.
True beauty in a woman is reflected in her soul. It's the caring
that she lovingly gives, the passion that she shows and the
beauty of a woman only grows with passing years.

Audrey Hepburn

ELEANOR

I was invited early last October to a birthday party. Not an ordinary birthday party, but certainly the most meaningful one that I've ever attended. For you see, this was a celebration of eighty years of life, the life of a true Matriarch, whose children recognize her significance in the forming of their lives and their children's lives.

Eleanor is the *Granna* to my dearest friend. But because of the distance, I had only met her a few times over the course of my friendship with her granddaughter, until this special day.

Eleanor has always been a *significant* person, in that her presence affects you. Perhaps it's the paradox of her manner, which can be both gentle and strong in the same moment. Or could it be the way her conversations, often laced with humor, contain the wisdom of the ages? Eleanor recognizes the value of her life and the life of all other living creatures. She has not wasted her life experiences by complaining, but rather by learning their lessons and passing them on through example rather than with mere words.

Eleanor has suffered, as all of us who live on this earth have suffered, but unlike many of us, she touches lives with grace, dignity and genuine caring. From the little I've observed, and all I have been told, Eleanor honors the *light*, both within herself and others. And so it was on that gorgeous day in San Francisco that a celebration of love was bestowed on her.

I hadn't attended with the notion that the experiences of that day would be remembered within the pages of my book. But the affection for this woman and the power of her legacy so touched me that I felt compelled to set it down on the mighty page in the hope you would find the same inspiration for your life.

Around two o'clock on a glorious sun-kissed San Francisco afternoon, the family and invited friends began arriving at the home of Eleanor's middle son, Jonathan. Though Eleanor's spirit remains strong, her health sometimes fails her, and the decision was made to celebrate at Jonathan's home rather than at a hotel. The backdrop of this beautiful home was ideal for the intimacy that unfolded. How inspiring to watch four generations reminiscing together as Eleanor, the common thread of their heritage, continued to weave them together with her warmth.

Despite such gracious hospitality, I felt like an outsider in a way, for only those who had shared the common wealth of this uncommon woman, and had the wisdom woven through her life shape their thoughts and values in so many ways, could truly revel in the joy of their shared memories. What was most obvious was how her family genuinely cherished their Mother, Grandmother and Great-Grandmother.

To begin the festivities, there were pictures drawn in crayon presented by the little ones to their *Great Granna*, and a few precious poems expressing their feelings for her. Then the older ones joined with them for a chorus of songs that had once been taught by the Birthday Girl to her children, so long ago.

Spider songs and lullabies, even an old, forgotten Christmas carol transported Eleanor back in her memories to a time long past. As the afternoon unfolded, and tears mingled with laughter, we all shared the pure reverence of this very special celebration.

But the best of all was saved for last. Eleanor's four children, now in their late fifties and early sixties, had each written a personal letter of favorite memories of their Mother. My expectation was that David, the eldest, would present these four poignant letters to their Mother ~ each a token of a grown-up child's love, written in perfect calligraphy and complimented by dark mahogany frames. And, indeed, David did hand the four letters to Eleanor. These letters were then passed around the room for each of us to share. I have never read sentiments so beautiful. I had the overwhelming sensation that I was reading, watching, and experiencing what the whole world longs for ~ to *belong*.

Following the presentation of the letters, the tribute continued as David and each of his siblings produced from under the dining room table several more framed copies of their own letters. These framed letters were then passed to each of their children as eternal reminders of the legacy their grandmother had gifted to each of them. Witnessing these letters being passed to the next generations, I realized the deep significance of what was happening within this loving family. I saw how in those letters, and on that extraordinary day in their lives, the truest gift to Eleanor was the gift of remembrance. Blessed be.

It is her compassion, laughter and wisdom that draws people, young and old, to Eleanor. What is unseen, hidden within her core, and learned long ago through the consequences of youth's poor choices, is her discernment when choosing who she invites into her inner circle. Ultimately, taking responsibility to protect her own soul is the truest lesson she has given to all of us, for loving herself is the light that leads her life.

I hate flowers. I paint them because they're cheaper than models and don't move.

Georgia O'Keefe

To commemorate your journey, your own *Wild Child* is invited to play with crayons and clay, and anything else your heart desires! *Journey Art* represents your life now lived with your eyes wide open. Your creation validates your new life through your tangible, visible, touchable affirmation of your power to create the life you want and deserve. Most importantly, your art gives voice to your child within to safely bring forward the feelings you feared to acknowledge or reveal before your journey. In the process, you trust your intuitive knowing as you create your unique outward expression of your inner reality.

Creative minds are rarely tidy. Creativity ~ like human life itself ~ begins in darkness.

Julia Cameron

Your artistic ability is immaterial. Through your creative process, even your crudest attempt, done mindfully, expresses something precious as you tap into what is unique and personal within you. For each of us, art comes from the intuitive *feeling* brain ~ the truest part of you ~ so the very act of creating brings forth what is most sacred within you.. There are no rules, no right way to create, so create as wild and crazy, as powerful and beautiful as you feel. For those of you thinking, *I've never been good at art,* this is your chance to step beyond that self-imposed limitation and open your creative soul! Just take that first step and you will find your artistic voice.

Anxiety is part of creativity, the need to get something out, the need to be rid of something or to get in touch with something within.

David Duchovny

133

As the creator, you are solely responsible for interpreting your own artwork. No one may impose a particular meaning on your piece. Only you will know the deepest, truest meaning of what you create. Whatever medium you choose, and how long the experience, the woman you are will find her expression in the right and perfect time.

Ideas to get You Started

The more meaningful your creation, the more the process of creating will both heal and celebrate all that makes you *you*. So please, first take the time to visualize *what* you want to express. You may want to sketch an image, or write a list of what you want your art to emphasize, or hum a few bars of the song coming in. The important part is your vision. Once you've decided on the *what*, then determine the *how*. If you need suggestions, the following list is there to help.

Medium suggestions: Clay, cloth, paper, paper mache, yarn, string, feathers, rocks, shells, song, poem, ceramics, wood, glass, photography, video.

Sketch, draw, sculpt, write or paint:

A series of self-portraits or images reflecting your outward and inward personas

A series of images reflecting your past, present and future

A picture or image that represents an issue of your journey

A series of pictures or images of who sat at your dinner table at different ages in your childhood

A mask that mirrors your inner self, or some aspect of yourself that you want to integrate

A poem, song, or original quotation

An artistic creation of a quotation that holds special meaning to your journey, childhood, or other significant event

A dream catcher or wall hanging

A patchwork quilt representing significant events in your life

A timeline to mark your life's major events and turning points

An expression of your history with your family, with sex, with faith, or with another major issue you have faced.

An expression of how you want your future to be

A collage of pictures, quotes and/or mementos

The Creative Adult is the Child Who Survived
Anonymous

Since the dawn of time artists have known intuitively what research is just now discovering ~ art is one of the most powerful tools to heal the human heart. Why? Because art needs no words to heal all that lies hidden within.

In Chapter 7, you learned the power of your words, however even words have their limits. Sometimes trauma can't be described with mere words. There simply is no vocabulary to adequately describe the depth of horror and pain of a true violation of the human spirit, especially within the innocence of a child's heart.

Words are irrelevant when your brain shifts from frontal lobe *thinking* to the place that holds all of your fear-based emotions as images ~ your limbic brain. Art gives form to your feelings. Your art is the most direct route to touch upon and shift those painful, crippling emotions into images with the power to heal your pain.

I found I could say things with color and shapes that
I couldn't say any other way ~ things I had no words for.
Georgia O'Keefe

As you create, you build an environmental *safe zone* around you. In that place, you can express emotions, cope with loss, and touch your deepest truths. At the same time, your brain replaces stress-based hormones with calming oxytocin and serotonin. That hormonal cocktail benefits your whole nervous system as the hours simply disappear, and so does life on the *outside.* In those hours of grace, you and your art are all that there is. So, go into your space, shut the door and invite in your goals and hopes, thoughts and feelings, joys and sorrows longing for expression.

In Preparation for Crossing the Bridge

The next chapters equip you with the tools you will need to walk into a world that all too often lacks understanding and respect for women, especially an empowered woman like you. Before you cross the Bridge, I encourage you to review your Journey Journal to remember how far you have actually travelled in learning the lessons of:

- Your father's and/or mother's influence
- Shifting *Should* to *What pleases me*
- Your truth behind every *I don't know*
- Confronting controllers
- Observing potential prince candidates
- Living your truth
- Trusting your intuition
- Contrasting *denial* with *Dignity*
- Treasuring your sisterhood
- Staying true to your values and goals
- Completing any other thoughts in your Journey Journal

As the first steps of your journey are behind you, remember to journal any new thoughts, plans or goals that come to mind. Check in with your mirror often to look into those beautiful eyes of yours and remind yourself of the one who loves you most.

JOURNEY JOURNALING:

What is my commitment to loving me first?

What are my immediate goals?

What steps do I take now to reach my current and future goals?

What support do I need from others to achieve these goals?

How do I plan to CELEBRATE my journey?

What might I create to COMMEMORATE my journey?

What thoughts do I have about crossing the Bridge?

MIRROR MAGIC: *I love you.*

Note:

Chapter 12 marks the end of your journey into *ME*, including the suggestions for your Mirror Magic exercise. I urge you to use your newfound self-awareness to continue this *I to I* time, creating your own messages to serve you, however you need in that particular time.

RECOMMENDED READS:

Drawing on the Right Side of Your Brain by Betty Edwards

The Zen of Creativity: Cultivating Your Artistic Life by John Loori

Cracking Creativity: The Secrets of Creative Genius by Michael Michalko

Nothing Special: Living Zen by Charlotte J. Beck and Steve Smith

A woman in harmony with her spirit is like a river flowing.
She goes where she will without pretense and arrives at her
destination prepared to be herself and only herself.

Maya Angelou

PART II

The BRIDGE

From Woman to the World Beyond

13 *Biology of Bonding:*
Neuropsychobiology for Dummies

Our brains remember, always, our first love,
and seek for it, again. The man to his mother,
the woman to her father. Nothing alters the brain
or body as much as being or not being loved.
Author Unknown

Our Terms:

BIOLOGY: The scientific study of living organisms in all its forms and developmental processes.

BONDING: A relationship of ongoing mutual attachment between parent and child that begins at birth and establishes the basis for all other relationships.

In the Antarctic, every March since the dawn of time,
the penguins' quest to find the perfect mate and start a family will
begin with a long journey ~ a journey that will take them hundreds
of miles across the continent by foot,
in freezing cold temperatures, in brittle, icy winds and through
deep, treacherous waters.
Penguins will risk starvation and attack by dangerous predators,
under the harshest conditions on earth, all to find true love.
Luc Jacquet ~ March of the Penguins

So, how is it that Mother Nature can guide thousands of adorable penguins safely through blizzards, sleet and frozen tundra on their way to find their perfect mate who is waiting patiently on the other side of the continent, and already thoughtfully attired for their wedding in tux-edo and tails, while you she leaves to meander in an endless maze as potential princes turned frogs trample hardened ruts in your heart? No wonder you can hear those little voices in your head debating the merits of *Thelma and Louise* or *Nice secluded convent*? *Thelma and Louise* or *Nice secluded convent?*

If our Good Mother would simply point you vaguely in his direction, you would gladly take it from there. As your dainty feet stepped onto the frozen tundra, with howling winds chafing your face, your heart would grow wings, your resolve would be clear. Hunger, bah! Treacherous waters, bah! Fighting off predators, no coffee lattes, bah! You would climb every mountain, forge every stream, follow every rainbow, knowing at journey's end his waiting arms will enfold you and never let you go. So will someone please get the word to Mother that you just need some direction here, preferably without detours? You have taken enough detours. You have kissed enough frogs!

Oh, Romeo, Romeo! Wherefore art thou, Romeo?
William Shakespeare

The timeless appeal of *Romeo and Juliet* comes as humanity's response to Shakespeare's brilliant window on our common longing to belong. Just as those two timeless lovers were caught in love's web, we also spend our lives wandering and wondering, caught up in its mystery, its paradox.

Thankfully, Mother Nature saw to it that loving and being loved would be the strongest forces of the human condition because belonging ensures her first priority: the survival of our species. Hence, your need to belong is stronger than even your need for food and shelter. The good news is that this means you're not crazy for wanting to love and to be loved. You're actually quite normal! But finding love at any cost is not. Yes, you are driven to bond because every cell in your body screams this is what is supposed to happen. But, oh ~ one more question ~ what about the excruciating pain when bonding falls apart?

When you put your life on hold waiting for the phone to ring or to see his face at your door, you are confronting nothing less than your primal evolutionary programming. When you try the singles bar just one more time, or sacrifice hours online in search of your illusive prince, or endure any sort of violation by a significant other, you're being driven by your innate desperation to belong. Failure to honor this essential force can be devastating. The reverse is also true. When one has endured relationship crashing as a way of life, the painfully obvious question *Why?* demands an answer. Thank goodness, there is one.

Your first step in making sense of the nonsense of 21st century dating is to understand that the quality of your earliest relationships programmed your brain, and his, for grown-up intimacy...or not. Admittedly, Mother Nature began with rather primitive requirements for family bonding. Take for example, reptiles, whose offspring arrive by egg. Pre-or post-hatching, *Mommy Dearest* either eats them alive or leaves them to their fate by simply slithering into the sunset. Not much bonding there. Not much brain either. The reptilian brain neither thinks nor feels. (I know what you're thinking ~ some men could qualify in this category ~ but let's get on with our story).

Over the next few 100 million years or so, as brains expanded, so did the quality of bonding between mates and their offspring. The earliest mammals evolved with a very primitive limbic brain, which gave them an enormous step up from the reptiles in the ability to actually *feel* emotion. Granted, this early brain had a rather short emotional list, namely FEAR for its survival. But delving more deeply into the limbic brain's significance, today's medical students learn to classify its functions as the Famous Four F's: **Feeding, Fighting, Fleeing and... sexually reproducing.**

Ah, but leave it to clever Mother Nature to know there had to be something even more wonderful than the Four F's! With another few 100 million years, the amazing limbic brain was overlaid with the even more amazing neocortex (the thinking brain), and nature was on its way to L*O*V*E*. From that point on, mating and maternal instincts took a quantum leap, developing an ever-more-elaborate courting ritual, followed by longer pregnancies and lactation, and laser-focused protection of vulnerable offspring. Eventually, the human brain would be gifted with the unique ability to shower our beloved mate and children with the language of love, such as in music, poetry, love letters, lullabies and whispered sweet nothings in the night. But again, back to our story.

Mammals, especially the higher-evolved primates, bond in mutually nurturing social groups, with plenty of touching, rubbing, nibbling, prancing, preening and shameless cavorting. These behaviors naturally lead to more involved bonding, which often results in babies who attach like glue to their mothers to be nursed, protected and nurtured until capable of fending for themselves.

It turns out that the critical key to survival of higher-ordered species is to fulfill the infant's biological desperation for parents to stay in close proximity to baby. In humans, such early and consistent bonding fulfills our life's first and most crucial task, to learn it is safe to *trust*.

How well the infant brain learns to trust his parents will build the platform for all intimate relationships to follow. (Would that be important information for you to know when choosing your prince?)

From the moment of birth your biological desperation to survive made you vulnerable to the people who made you. Mother Nature planned long ago that little ones are to be protected by the big ones, so she didn't give your baby brain the ability to handle stress. Rather, as an infant, your sense of safety and survival depended on feeling safe in their arms, as in knowing your protectors were close enough to protect you.

To ensure bonding, and thus the survival of our species, Mother Nature created the perfect plan. When a human mother holds her newborn skin to skin, especially in the first two hours following birth, her brain synchronizes with her baby's brain in a shared overdose of oxytocin and serotonin ~ the hormones of love and peace. (This last sentence is such a profound statement you might want to reread it). This brain state of *baby bliss* is nature's brilliant idea for bonding the mother-child relationship for life. In this brief window of time, bonding hormones cause the mother to fall so deeply in love with her infant that her brain becomes hard-wired to protect him or her with an even greater fierceness than a mother bear will protect her cub.

Your female brain knows quite well the intensity of these very same hormones. When you believe you've found your prince, it is oxytocin that takes your emotions to euphoria with just the thought of him. When he loves you in return, serotonin joins the mix, and your shared sense that it's safe to trust the other harmonizes your chemicals in what scientists call *emotional resonance*. Needless to say, blending serotonin and oxytocin makes quite a love cocktail! Ever hear of being drunk on love? Well, it is way better than anything out of a bottle or can!

For the infant, mother's love is even better. Her consistent nurturing imprints on the baby's brain the first impression of his new world. Their shared *love* hormones set the baby-brain wiring in preparation for later emotional intimacy, which builds the family foundation so the cycle of life will continue. However, if their hormonal love fest is interrupted, nature's perfect plan takes a detour. If the mother is physically and/or emotionally distant, the baby's limbic brain senses a disabling threat to its own survival, replacing the bonding hormones with cortisol ~ the stress hormone. You can relate such panic to the times you feared the man you deeply loved was slipping away from your life. Your limbic brain assaulted you with survival questions like *How can I live without him?* Somehow, you muddled through the grief and started over. But, for a baby, when bonding collapses, his brain answers this most legitimate question with a deathly terror that will weave through life into his future intimate relationships.

So, it all boils down to chemistry, that word we toss around as we decide if love is really love. Ironically, once upon our earliest days, chemistry was literally all that mattered. Chemistry set the course in our brains that set the course of our lives.

In your first 1,000 days, you were more vulnerable physically and emotionally than at any other stage of your life. Before you developed language ~ around your third birthday ~ you couldn't truly think or reason, as both require language. Also, without language, you could only express yourself with primitive emotions. Without language, you could not rationalize why Mommy didn't come when you cried. You couldn't predict that in two minutes (forever on *baby time*) she'd be picking you up and wiping your tears away. Your only frame of reference was whatever you experienced in the moment, without any means to understand what was happening to you, or why. As you *felt* each experience, your primitive, pure emotions took root in your limbic *feeling* brain with your first, most crucial impressions of being human. *Safe or scared?* (Clinical term: Anxiety). *Happy or sad?* (Clinical term: Depression).

The Quality of Parenting Determines the Ultimate Nature of The Child's Mind

Children raised in a consistent, secure, and joy-filled family enjoy the greatest chance to grow into self-confident adults who are flexible, creative, hopeful, optimistic, and able to embrace the emotional intimacy required of conscious relationship. Because of the strong foundation their parents built beneath them, as they mature they are able to ebb and flow with life's difficulties.

In comparison, an early life of connect/disconnect, attach/detach, bond/separate parenting interrupts normal emotional development. In clinical terms, this lack of early consistency is known as *insecure attachment.* As the child grows, the unpredictability of his earliest, most vulnerable relationship, most often with his primary connection to his mother, now creates an unconscious war of psychic survival between *fear of abandonment* versus *fear of not belonging*; *fear of love* versus *fear of losing love*. In this double-bind dilemma, the unnatural fear of intimacy overrides the natural longing to bond. As this child matures, his or her fractured soul has no significant experience or limbic programming as to what love even looks or feels like. The chances for the child to have any true success at adult intimacy are extremely poor.

We are born with the need to be loved, and never outgrow it.
Helen Keller

When one's childhood was fear-based, it's not hard to imagine that the mere thought of future intimacy would strike terror within. Imagine this monologue playing out in one's brain: *I'm so lonely, but if I decide to love someone they will abandon me. But I'm deathly afraid of being alone. Without someone I won't survive. But if I decide to care for someone they will abandon me. So I will sabotage them before they sabotage me. But I'm afraid ~ deathly afraid ~ of being alone.*

Such push-pull craziness creates adult dynamics of rigid *black and white* thinking, self-medicating addictions, power and control struggles, overt rage, passive-aggressiveness, introversion, pessimism, narcissism, suspiciousness, lying, and impulsivity, and every bit of it is dictated by primal fear. How tragic that the most intricate, complex, miraculous, transcendent creation, the human brain evolving over millions, perhaps billions of years, can be so easily tripped up by emotional neglect suffered in the first 1,000 days of its life. Tripped up, but not destroyed.

Wise Women Have Noted That Knowledge is Power

Perhaps this chapter has shed light on why suffering has been such a part of the lives of your friends, family, lovers, maybe even your own. But is life's longing for love doomed to fail forever because of the failure of others? Thankfully, the answer is *No*. Research supports that positive, self-nurturing choices can change our brain, rewiring neural pathways and transforming limbic patterns of *cortisol panic* into peace. When one courageously chooses such deep reprogramming, the childhood wounds that have sabotaged any hope of trusting another human being, the core of intimate relationships, can begin to heal.

You have taken the courage to confront your most wrenching pain; to trust yourself first; to know who you truly are and what you truly deserve; to choose to nurture your health, your heart, your thoughts and your dreams. This self-loving releases within your brain a flood of oxytocin and serotonin to 100 billion thirsty brain cells. These hormones have the power to regenerate the life force that is greater than even nature's power to push a fragile flower through asphalt! It's called love, and your courage to take this journey has already made it happen within you…

JOURNEY JOURNALING:

What do I now understand about bonding and the brain?

How do I remember my early home environment?

What three adjectives describe my mother? What three adjectives describe my father?

What three adjectives describe my earliest home life?

How does this information change my thinking about my childhood?

RECOMMENDED READS:

Homecoming: Reclaiming and Healing Your Inner Child
by John Bradshaw

Family Secrets: The Path from Shame to Healing
by John Bradshaw

A General Theory of Love by Drs. Lewis, Amini, and Lannon

The Continuum Concept: In Search of Happiness Lost
by Jean Liedloff

Toxic Parents: Overcoming Their Hurtful Legacy and Reclaiming Your Life by Susan Forward

TOUCHING: The Human Significance of Skin
by Ashley Montague

Becoming Attached: First Relationships and How They Shape Our Capacity to Love by Robert Karen, Ph.D.

RECOMMENDED DVD'S:

March of the Penguins, Alliance de Production Cinematographique

The Weeping Camel, Think Film Production in alliance with National Geographic

On Becoming NaughtABimbeaux

14 *Analyze This!*
Reading the Handwriting on the Wall,
or Maybe Just on a Nice Cocktail Napkin

Every man has something he can do better than anyone else.
Usually, it is reading his own handwriting.
Unknown

Dating without using handwriting analysis is like playing poker
with your eyes closed. You might draw a losing hand or a
winning hand... but you won't know the difference.
Bart A. Baggett

Our Terms:

ANALYZE: Determine the elements or essential features; to examine critically and in detail, so as to identify causes, key factors, possible results; understand the essential elements or give the essence of.

GRAPHOLOGY: The study of handwriting, especially when regarded as yielding clues to the writer's character.

MARGARET

Even though they had dated for only four months, because he said he loved her more than life itself, Margaret said *Yes* to marry the most wonderful man she'd ever known. He was so eager that she carry his name, he urged her to marry him the very next month. He told her that would give them enough time to get their finances in order. Actually, it gave him time to assess her finances, and then decide how much of her money he could *borrow* to fund his next new business scheme.

As they stood at the altar, if Margaret could have seen into his soul she would have known he was lying with every word of every vow. Unfortunately, all she could see into were his baby blue eyes looking straight down into hers as he whispered *I love you* before he, a bonafide conman, sealed their union with a kiss. Three decades later, Margaret would still remember that was the last time she ever saw *love* in his eyes.

After ending their thirteen-year marriage from hell, what he did love ~ her father's inheritance ~ was not Margaret's anymore. In fact, it didn't even exist. He had spent every dime looking like a big fish in a small pond, then left her with debt on her own inheritance. Dipping into her meager savings, she hired a therapist who introduced her to the word **sociopath**. Finally, dear Margaret *got it*. All those years, while she was naively making love to make a family, he had been f_ _ _ing her for her fortune.

Carrying her father's rage from his grave, Margaret fought back. She used the little money she had left to hire an attorney to file a judgment against him. She won. It was then she saw the fury in his eyes and felt the threat in his voice as he yelled in her face, *Screw the judgment. I'm filing bankruptcy. You'll never see a cent.* He had no intention of ever paying her back what he had *borrowed*. Arriving in bankruptcy court the following year, Margaret witnessed dozens of other creditors walk away with some monetary compensation, as they could offer the Court signed loan documents from years before. But, since Margaret was an *unsecured creditor* ~ meaning: *just a wife* whose greatest mistake was that she had trusted her husband ~ all of his years of worthless promises to repay her meant, according to U.S. Bankruptcy Code 11, he owed her nothing. Once the dust settled from the Judge's judgment, Margaret realized she was destitute. In other words, this time **she** lost. For him, winning was never the goal. Not losing was. There's a difference.

After Margaret's divorce, she qualified for a scholarship to earn her business degree. Three years later that degree won her an interview with a local company. Her integrity and contagious sparkle helped her secure the position. As she worked her way up through the ranks, she soon met a man from the corporate office who made his interest known. After dating for several months, Margaret's ex-husband's betrayal still kept her heart from believing all of this new man's sweet words.

Even when her response to his advances could not possibly be misread, he remained true to meeting her every need without asking anything in return. He was willing to wait for her to fall in love with him, no matter how long it took. Finally, after four years of his kindness and generosity, Margaret questioned her intuition. Was she passing up her one opportunity for true love? Even though they had little in common, and she certainly felt no chemistry, *Maybe*, she thought, *I've never known real love. Maybe, I just don't recognize it when it is staring me in the face.* So Margaret said *Yes* for the second time and turned her life towards his.

The one thing that Margaret didn't know about him was the one thing he purposefully kept hidden: his childhood. What Margaret was turning towards was the hidden agenda of a damaged son's *mother rage.* He had arranged the timing, the strategy and the finesse to insure her soul would bleed. Once Margaret lived under his roof, and behind closed doors, the pain of his past erupted with such intensity that Margaret literally ran for her life, following the footsteps of his three previous wives.

> *It's amazing that companies will pay headhunters thousands of dollars on finding the right vice president, but some people won't invest 80 bucks and ten minutes to make sure they're choosing the right life-long partner.*
> Bart A. Baggett

A second divorce and two years later, Margaret had been promoted to Personnel Director of her company. She knew that hiring the right people was the number-one priority to keep a company successful. When her boss had her attend training on *graphology*, Margaret's mind went on double track as she listened. She learned that graphology is a documented study of handwriting analysis. It is used throughout the world as an objective tool for recognizing the full spectrum of personality traits. Eighty percent of French companies use it in their hiring practices. Even the FBI has developed computer programs to assess handwriting of serial killers, rapist, and terrorists.

If studying handwriting on an employment questionnaire could reveal personality traits necessary for a certain job position, why not apply the same in her search for a man she could really love, and most importantly, trust? After all, if the FBI trusts graphology enough to solve cases of national security, why wouldn't she use it for her own personal security?

When offered a free analysis at the end of the training, Margaret stood first in line. She was amazed how accurately the trainer could *see* her personality in her writing. Intrigued, she attended a second training and was *hooked.* With a few classes and more practice, Margaret's skills became so accurate that friends started bringing her the writing samples of their significant others. Margaret had become the *Graphology Guru!*

Armed with her new skill, there came the day her heart had known would eventually need to happen. Margaret took a very deep breath, looked in her mirror and whispered *I love you,* then opened the kitchen door to her garage. She started searching through the boxes, hunting for the one labeled *Financial Documents, 1980-1990.* She spied it up on the top shelf. As she took another deep breath, Margaret climbed the ladder, then pulled it down onto the floor. She carefully pulled back the lid and started rummaging through papers that had yellowed over the two decades that had passed since she had last looked on them.

Then, in the next moment, she felt as if the air she breathed was being sucked out of her lungs. There it was. Their marriage license. His signature. She saw with new eyes his pathology glaring up at her in the ego and anger signs in his rushed *can't be bothered* scribble of a signature. She didn't know whether to laugh or cry. Had she known then what she knew now, that *tell all* signature would've sent her running from his bogus proposal of wedded bliss so many wrenching years before.

She leaned against her car, feeling the wet tears on her cheeks. He had pursued her not to love her, but to use her. He had mocked and murdered every childhood dream she'd ever had about love, marriage and family. With cold calculation, devoid of any conscience, he had profaned the most sacred of relationships as he laughed all the way to the bank. He had raped her soul for money. As Margaret put that worthless paper back on the pile, and started to close the box, like a ghost from the past she heard his voice saying those words that, in retrospect, became the only truth he ever told her. *Don't think I'll ever pay you a cent. I'll go bankrupt first.*

His lies had taken away everything but her spirit to thrive. She now knew that such a betrayal would never happen to her again. Never again would she trust mere spoken words that could hide an agenda that could cut her heart out of her chest and leave her to bleed. Analyzing written words, she could *cut to the chase* in seconds rather than years. Graphology would protect her soul while looking for love and the one to share it with.

Handwriting is Actually Brain Writing

There are 99 primary traits revealed in the way one writes. The impulses required to write words are generated within the brain. Since the brain holds the subconscious memories of our childhoods, and has wired our personality traits and survival strategies, as we write, those neural impulses translate into our handwriting. How a person forms their letters and combines those letters into words reveals a unique profile of their personality traits.

To their credit, men do not decorate their penmanship.
They just chicken-scratch.

Women use scented, colored stationary and they
dot their "i's" with circles and hearts. Women use ridiculously
large loops in their "p's" and "g's."

It is a royal pain to read a note from a woman.
Even when she's dumping you, she'll put a smiley face
at the end of the note."
Author Unknown

You can Know in Seconds if a Man is Safe

Handwriting reveals the core of a man within thirty seconds of the time he puts his pen to paper. Not only will you know immediately if this man is worthy of walking you down the aisle, just as importantly, you will know if he is worthy of walking you to your car!

When meeting that new gentleman can offer the potential of fantasy or fatality, would you appreciate having the ability to know which way he leans in a few seconds rather than months or even years?

You are standing on the threshold of living your power as *NaughtA-Bimbeaux* in the world beyond your front door. Learning Graphology's simple 7 Danger Signs builds your self-confidence as you now know how to *read* writing. Easily and quickly, you will discern ~ for your own well-being ~ who is frog and who is prince; who is *fraud* and who is *Forever.*

Graphology Indicators of the 7 Danger Signs

Graphology's 7 Danger Signs equip you with a tool that predicts if a potential mate has tendencies towards lying, depression, stubbornness, argumentativeness, aggressiveness, emotional withdrawal, need to dominate, sense of entitlement, sarcasm, and/or violence. These 7 signs reveal hidden agendas when all he wants to reveal is the sparkling tip of a deeply submerged and very cold iceberg.

Shown by hard right upstrokes that replace a lower loop. The aggressive person pushes forward into the future, asserting himself physically. Often this person needs physically aggressive outlets such as competitive sports or even violence.

aggressive

Shown by a combination of loops in the right and left side of lower case a's and o's. Inner loops that cross signify a person that is not comfortable telling the whole truth. The bigger the loops, the bigger the lies.

lying

Shown by a stinger-like hook in the middle zone letters c, d, or a. This person has an anger at strong members of the opposite sex, while only being attracted to those who are a challenge. Once this person feels totally in control of the relationship, he/she will become bored.

issues with opposite sex

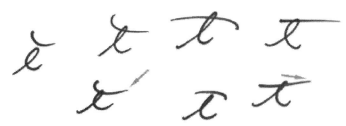

Revealed by a sharp-pointed t-bar. Sarcasm is like a verbal dagger defending the ego. Sarcasm is forming a dual meaning to whatever is said and is often mixed with humor. Sarcastic people have a sharp tongue that can hurt other's feelings.

sarcasm

Shown by the large looped stem in the lower case d or t. The bigger the loop, the more painful criticism will feel. If the loop is really inflated, this person will imagine criticism. The d-loop relates to appearance, and the t-loop relates to sensitivity about ideas or philosophies.

sensitive to criticism

Revealed by t and d stems shaped like a teepee or upside down "V". The more this letter is braced, the more this person is braced to defend his own ideas. Stubborn people have a fear of being wrong, and don't want to be confused with the facts after they have made up their minds.

stubborn

hot temper t-bar

Shown by a t-bar that is crossed predominantly on the right side of the stem. The more it occurs, the easier irritation will cause them to lose control of their emotions. If combined with a heavy right slant, they will blow up quickly when under stress.

temper

The **7 Danger Signs** contain a thimble-full of an ocean of the study of graphology. Every other trait you can imagine, from how fast he drives and how he manages money to how he feels about his mother, are all there on the page.

Bart Baggett's Handwriting Analysis Training Course is considered an industry leader. www.handwritinguniversity.com This site gives the entire Catalog of DVDs, CDs, Videos, Home Study Courses & Books by Bart Baggett. Sign up for Bart's free weekly Graphology Newsletter PLUS get the Free Handwriting Special report.

JOURNEY JOURNALING:

How will I use this information?

Whose handwriting am I most curious to analyze? Why?

How would certain relationships have been different had I known this information earlier in my life?

What are my thoughts on learning graphology?

RECOMMENDED READS:

Handwriting Analysis 101 by Bart A. Baggett

Change Your Handwriting, Change Your Life by Bart A. Baggett

The Secrets to Making Love Happen by Bart A. Baggett

Handwriting Analysis: Secrets of Love, Sex and Relationships
by Bart A. Baggett

Handwriting Analysis: Putting It to Work for You
by Andrea McNichol

Handwriting Analysis: The Complete Basic Book by Karen Amend
& Mary S. Ruiz

Special *Thank You* to Bart Baggett of MyHandwriting.com for permission to duplicate his examples of the 7 Danger Sign graphics. Mr. Baggett has been featured on the TV Show, *America's Most Wanted*, where he performed analysis of handwriting styles and personality disorders.

PART III

HE

The Relevance of Research When Choosing One's Prince

15 *I Finally Got It:*
Men Don't Get It
& That's Just the Way It Is

If it has tires or testicles, you're gonna have trouble with it.
Ms. Anonymous

It's so nice to have a man around the house.
Just don't let him inside, that's when all the trouble starts.
Ms. Anonymous

Our Terms:

MAN: An adult male person, as distinguished from a boy or a woman; the nature, characteristics, or feelings often attributed to men; manliness.

WOMAN: The female human being; the nature, characteristics, or feelings often attributed to women; womanliness.

DIFFERENT: Not alike in character or quality; differing; dissimilar: not identical; separate or distinct.

DAVID

Little David's mom had made a conscious commitment to buy no toy guns or allow violent TV shows or violent video games in their home. She modeled compassion to her son at every turn. She saw to it that David's favorite toys were Raggedy Andy, Snoopy, wooden blocks and a couple of match-box cars. His favorite book? *The Little Engine that Could.*

One frosty Sunday morning in December, David and his parents met up with family after church for lunch at a local restaurant. With the Christmas-themed Sunday School lesson fresh on his three-year-old mind, David, with the face of a cherub, approached his newborn cousin innocently resting in her infant seat, cocked his finger in her face, and calmly, but with his *outside* voice, shouted ***Pow Pow, Baby Jesus!!***

Here's another example of our differences and, for obvious reasons, will remain anonymous:

A wife overheard her husband relay this information to a friend on the phone. *You know how when you're peeing at home, aiming into the bowl? And you see a little smudge of poop in the bowl from earlier and you aim for it and make it go away? I really feel like I'm helping out when I do that, like Hey! I just cleaned the bathroom.*

And another ~ to explain why they never listen: It has been told to generations past that when God creates little boys, before He sends them down to earth, He asks each one which option he prefers ~ penis or ears? Each little fellow only gets to choose one.

Even Our Best Intentions Cannot Overrule Biology

Ever wonder why men are, you know, so impossible? Why is it that just when your relationship sweetens, he turns sour? Or why, after you've just shared, for the first time in your life, your most deeply guarded secret, he blinks twice and asks for another beer? And, what is it about wasting an absolutely beautiful day in front of the TV with the NFL, NBA, MLB, PGA, NHL, NSL or XYZ?

Many a French lover has sung the praises of *Viva Le Difference.* Who are they kidding? *Viva Le Difference* makes you crazy! In the Broadway musical, *My Fair Lady,* Professor Henry Higgins offered the question, *Why Can't a Woman be More Like a Man?* If the Professor was still around today, science would hand him the answer on a silver platter: It's our biology, Professor!

> **As long as you know men are like children,**
> **you know everything.**
> Coco Channel

In Chapter 13, The Biology of Bonding, you learned that the baby brain, regardless of gender, requires nurturing to program in one's ability to trust and nurture as we mature. Taking that reality to the next level, knowing the differences between the female and male brain provides us with the golden key to unlock the mystery of why men are, you know, the way they are. Both male and female brains are each an intricately complicated organ of around 100 billion neurons, divided into right and left hemispheres, each with unique, specialized functions. Their very extensive connecting system allows the hemispheres to *talk to each other* so each side can integrate impulses. Girl brains seem to do this better...quite a bit better.

Guys will be happy to learn that they have 4% more brain cells than women, and about 100 grams more brain tissue. However, even with our slightly smaller brain, we have the advantage of more wiring between our hemispheres. This *cross-wiring* allows both hemispheres to *talk* to each other. The advantages are that we use language more efficiently, can multitask without blowing a fuse, and can spark up *whole brain thinking* to see the big picture. In other words, in general we enjoy a much more efficient brain. It needs to be emphasized that these comments refer to the average male or female brain. There are, of course, many females who can outdo males on visual-spatial tasks, and many males who excel more than females in language abilities. As you likely know already, most men tend to focus on what's in front of them.

Chapter 13 described how our limbic brain is hidden deep inside the larger brain. There are definite gender differences to that one, as well. Men's brains are wired for fight or flight; ours for tend and befriend. Evidently, our tending and befriending requires more neural activity than fighting or fleeing, thus our limbic brains are larger and more highly developed. This probably explains why we are more in touch with our emotions, have a greater ability to express our feelings, and enjoy a natural ability to bond and feel connected to others. This may also explain why there has never been a society on earth where men replaced women as the primary caretakers of children.

The female brain is an easier brain to teach.
It's harder for the male brain to learn.
Michael Gurian

Compared to us strong, advanced baby girls, the vulnerability of little boys begins as early as in the womb. After five months of pregnancy, we females are already two weeks ahead of males developmentally. Even though more males are conceived, their numbers advantage lasts about as long as the candle on their first birthday cake, if they make it that far. If the woman carrying a boy experiences significant stress, her stress chemicals pass through the umbilical cord and compromise her unborn male's ability to survive to birth. If the little guy is not spontaneously aborted, he will be at greater risk of premature birth. If he does survive and is born full term, he enters the world at greater risk of brain damage, cerebral palsy and developmental delays. Since male embryos, fetuses and newborns are more likely to die prematurely, nature has compensated by skewing the birth rate in their favor ~105 males to 100 females.

At birth, even though fewer in number, we girls are now four weeks ahead in our overall development compared to boys. At a stunning 24 hours old, our newly opened eyes happily linger on the faces smiling at ours. Before our first day is over, we are already busy learning how to establish and maintain eye contact. Even though all newborns recognize their mother's voice within 24 hours after birth, we females are absolutely mesmerized by hers, and everyone else's! On that same first day, if given the opportunity, those brand new baby boy eyes will bypass those adoring faces, preferring to zero in on such fascinating objects as geometric mobiles. By his six month, the human face still won't hold the fascination offered by blinking lights, geometric patterns, colored photographs of objects and three-dimensional *whatevers.*

Give us females six months, and if we could talk we'd be demanding *More faces, more conversation, please. And keep it coming!* About the same time, our natural competency to read facial expressions is emerging. We will already show a higher degree of empathy to the distress of others than any future prince ever dreamed. As an example, at six months, when we hear another child cry we are much more likely to cry with them. Most baby boys couldn't care less about all that commotion. They are much more intrigued with being in motion!

Overall, and over time, we are just more aware and willing to respond to social cues. For instance, if Mommy smiles and nods towards an object we've never seen before, both boy and girl babies will reach out and touch it. However, if Mommy acts afraid of the object, we darlings take our cue, trust she knows best, and simply avoid it and get busy with something less threatening.

But, those boys will be boys. Who cares if Mommy's scared when there's opportunity for real adventure? Out go his little hands as his cherub face looks up into hers, all but daring her with the devil in his eyes...*Just try to stop me!*

By the time we're all toddling around the coffee table, baby girls continue to have radically different responses to crisis. When we notice someone in distress, we respond with compassion. Even though we lack the words, our facial expressions and gestures show our concern with a puzzled face that says, *How can I help?* When language does kick in, we ask questions such as *What wrong?* or *Me help?*

As the toddler boy's gross motor skills and three-dimensional processing outshines ours, he can't be bothered. After all, can't we see that his block tower is much more engrossing than all the silly ruckus of some baby crying?

Later, while we girls organize our doll houses ~ showing an impressive innate understanding of family as a system of give-and-take relationships ~ those boys are jumping off ladders with their Superman capes flapping in the breeze. For them, play equals themes of power, dominance and aggression. They like following *boys' rules* because those rules are designed to make them appear powerful, dominant, even *macho*. Where would *vulnerable* and *patient* fit into that list?

Since relating well to females of any age doesn't come naturally, by the time those boys are on their way to being men they tend to avoid all those messy relationship conversations we seem to want to bring up. How? By distracting themselves with problems that are easily solved, say for instance, fixing the car's windshield wiper or couch-coaching the next play of Monday Night Football! Rumor has it that at such a time as this, if the woman they love, even the mother of their children, walks in front of the TV stark naked, her *Honey* will look right through her as he hurls insults at the quarterback.

In contrast, we easily and naturally prefer to talk out our problems. We value being sensitive and maintaining good relationships ~ attachment over achievement. Hello? Are you catching the drift here? How many times have your relationships evolved from *Fantasy* to *Frustration* to *Finished* because expectations on both sides were out of touch with the reality of our innate gender differences?

As much as you may hope, and as hard as you might try, your typical Prince Charming really isn't equipped to understand, need, or seek emotional intimacy as the elixir of a relationship. This would be important information if keeping sane is anywhere near the top of your priority list!

Love is the history of a woman's life; it is an episode in man's.
Germaine de Stael

JOURNEY JOURNALING:

How does science answer my questions about men?

Given this information, what relationship expectations do I have that are unrealistic?

How might I meet my needs for conversation and companionship in the future?

RECOMMENDED READS:

The Dance of Intimacy by Harriet G. Lerner, Ph.D.

You Just Don't Understand: Women and Men in Conversation by Deborah Tannen

Why Can't You Read My Mind?: Overcoming the 9 Toxic Thought Patterns that Get in the Way of a Loving Relationship by Jeffrey Bernstein and Susan Magee

16 *Mr. Right vs. Mr. Right Now:*
The Joy of Mediocrity

If you limit your choices only to what seems possible or reasonable, you disconnect yourself from what you truly want, and all that is left is compromise.

Robert Fritz

Our Terms:

RIGHT: In conformity with fact, reason, truth, or some standard or principle; correct; the right solution; the right answer; correct in judgment, opinion, or action.

MEDIOCRE: Inferior; of only ordinary or moderate quality; neither good nor bad; barely adequate; undistinguished, common place, everyday; run-of-the-mill.

COMPROMISE: To weaken; to settle.

JENNIFER

Jennifer was married to Mr. Mediocre for twenty-five passionless years. His idea of romance was to creep up behind her and pinch her behind while she washed their dishes. What she longed for was his kiss on her neck. That one kiss could have kindled a flame that would've lasted through the night. She told him this, many times.

Mr. Mediocre's idea of foreplay was to yank back the shower curtain and wiggle his eyebrows at her now exposed naked body. Time and time again, what she longed for was a surprise bouquet of wildflowers. She would've given him anything he wanted in exchange for those flowers. She told him this too, many, many times.

Every anniversary and every birthday went by with not a word, much less a celebration. On a daily basis, he screamed at the kids to take out the trash, mow the grass and feed the dog while he sat drinking his beer on their fifteen-year-old couch. Then he had the nerve to think that after chasing three kids and their friends around the house, yard and neighborhood all day, by 10 PM Jennifer would be thrilled to jump into bed for an hour of *fun*…actually make that ten minutes, max. Oh, and *fun* is probably not the operative word either.

I danced naked for him. I played the harlot, the boarding school Head Mistress, and the Masochistic Mommy ~ whatever he wanted me to be so he could get off. I bore and raised his children without wasting my breath asking for his help, she would tell her friends. Of course, she also cooked his meals, washed his clothes, soothed his brow, rubbed his back and kissed his ass. Never once did she forget the things he didn't do for her, no matter how many times she'd asked.

Jennifer would have sacrificed her right arm to bring back the hours she spent trying to enjoy what he enjoyed, like fishing, throwing darts, bowling, even watching football. She would have given up her last dollar to have back the years of her life she invested to support his every scheme to *make it rich*. She would have given up her health to find the magical words that would actually get through to him, to make him understand about everything he stole from her.

> **The thing women have yet to learn is nobody gives you power.**
> **You just take it.**
> Roseanne Barr

There came the day when Jennifer finally woke up, and then gave up. She had debated for years about leaving because he had never hit her, or physically abused her or their children in any way. They had a roof over their heads and food in the fridge, but she was dying a slow death inside from the mediocrity, the blandness of it all. Surely that counted for something. She knew nothing would change if she didn't change. She would forever be *Mr. Mediocre's Mrs. Unappreciated* if she didn't stand up for the life she deserved. After all, being treated with just a bit of respect, and sharing hopes and dreams with the father of one's children didn't seem too much to ask. Oh, yes, and passion. Her body and heart ached to feel passion. Her mind knew she never would if she stayed.

So, she grabbed her children, a couple of suitcases, the little hope she had left, and made her move across town. Then, she filed for divorce. The whole process was agonizing, quite like their marriage had been before she saw to it that it was over.

> *The Queen had one way of settling all difficulties,*
> *great or small.*
> *'Off with his head!' she said, without even looking around.*
> Lewis Carroll

ELIZABETH

Elizabeth I of England was born September 7, 1533, in Greenwich Palace, the third child of King Henry VIII. When she was two years old, *Daddy* beheaded her mother, Ann Boleyn. Five years later, he married Catherine Howard, the first cousin to her mother. Even though Elizabeth loved Catherine, Henry had her beheaded before their second wedding anniversary. Young Elizabeth learned early of death, and too well, as still to come was the death of her father in 1547, and that of her brother, Edward VI. Then, as if that wasn't enough, the coronation of her Catholic half-sister, Mary I, began several religious rebellions and uprisings against her, a protestant adolescent female. Jealous and fearful of her little sister's popularity, Mary imprisoned Elizabeth in the Tower of London, with the threat of beheading as a constant terror. But, instead of Elizabeth's death, it was Mary's early demise that dramatically changed Elizabeth's life and all of world history. When Queen Mary died, young Elizabeth succeeded her to the throne of England. She was 25 years old.

> *All good is hard. All evil is easy. Dying, losing, cheating*
> *and mediocrity are easy. Stay away from easy.*
>
> Scott Alexander

Elizabeth I, a young and traumatized woman, was thrust into a position of power at a time of unimaginable political upheaval and religious opposition. Not only Elizabeth, but also her royal court, the warring Catholics and Protestants, and every citizen within the land knew full well that the young Queen's life was constantly in danger.

Of course, as a mere teenager who had always lived in fear for her life, Elizabeth felt overwhelmed. Not only was her emerging power raising the stakes even higher on her survival, but she alone carried the responsibility of ruling a kingdom as her enemies watched intently, waiting for her to fail. Her fear from this whole sticky situation was staggering, but she had no time to wallow in self-pity or emotional paralysis. She realized in choosing to rule England that she must also rule herself. She had to reach deep within herself to overcome her legitimate self-doubt, vulnerability and sheer terror. So then, what did she do? She set her sights on the prize, and shaking in her royal shoes **Elizabeth stood up**.

> *I know I have the body but of a weak and feeble woman;*
> *but I have the heart and stomach of a king;*
> *and of a king of England too.*
>
> Elizabeth I, Speech at Tilbury, 1588, England

From that place of seizing her power, the young Queen Elizabeth I ascended her throne to become one of the most powerful monarchs the world has ever known. Her reign was to become the longest in the history of England, to that time. **Her choice to remain true to herself did not allow the luxury of mediocrity.** Her choices reflected her determination to choose the extraordinary. Her choice to be brilliant as a woman unto herself literally catapulted her and England into unequaled power. Over the next forty-four years, Elizabeth's choice ~ to STAND ~ fueled her noble resolve to aim high to ensure she and her beloved England would reach their destiny.

I wish someone would've told me that, just because I'm a girl,
I don't have to get married.
Marlo Thomas

Perhaps it has occurred to you by now that your resolve to never kiss another frog may result in never kissing again. Perhaps you're thinking that such exclusiveness sets your bar a bit too high. If incomprehensible panic ensues as this point, the thought of compromise cannot be far behind.

No matter how love-sick a woman is, she shouldn't take
the first pill that comes along.
Dr. Joyce Brothers

So, are you actually thinking about settling for Mr. Right Now for right now? Really? Well, if that is what you're considering, let's review what all of us know already. The dating world is full of Mr. Right Nows. They can be really decent, hard-working, polite, generous men, or maybe they are not.

Despite my thirty years of research into the feminine soul, I have not
been able to answer the great question that has never been answered:
What does a woman want?
Sigmund Freud

For a woman, there is nothing more erotic
than to be understood.
Molly Haskell

Quite often, rather than looking at why they lose out in relationships, the Mr. Medicores complain that we expect too much, analyze too much, or complain (nag) too much. But, the truth is they are missing something. Maybe it's the vocabulary of intimacy, or knowing that open, respectful communication is crucial, or maybe they are just emotionally tone-deaf.

Trying our best to help these men understand, we women actually attempt to explain it to them. Big mistake! You already know that when you try to explain what he's missing…he misses the point. To be fair, he isn't doing anything actually wrong. He truly believes women just want too much, which, reading between the lines, we interpret to mean, *No woman wants to settle,* as in *marry me.* Mr. Mediocre is clueless, and trying to make him understand what we understand drains him and us. He takes our effort, and then fails to see he provides us no inspiration or passion in return. And, can we all agree with Jennifer that it is *passion* ~ especially the lingering looks and those naughty little secrets that only lovers share ~ that keep our love fires burning?

So, if you choose Mr. Right Now for right now, what you need to remember is:

1.) He is clueless about the depth and breadth of intimacy.

2.) Intimacy is what we came here for.

> ***It starts when you sink in his arms***
> ***and ends with your arms in his sink.***
> Author Unknown

But surely there will be those of us sisters, in spite of all you've faced and conquered in your journey, in spite of the passion you long for, who will still choose compromise. If this is you (and I do again have to ask, *Really?*), please don't compromise your integrity, too. At the very least, be upfront with him. Tell him exactly what your intentions are in dating him, or sleeping with him. Admit that you are marking time using his time. Admit that you don't see a future with him. **Keep your integrity.** Tell him the truth. And for goodness sakes, if he chooses to go, let him. And a BIG shout-out to you who will not compromise ever again because your one and only question going forward in your life is *Is he WORTHY of Me?*

> *Don't compromise yourself. You are all you've got.*
> Janis Joplin

Elizabeth I reigned with a discernment born from her intuition. To stay alive, *compromise* was not in her vocabulary. She learned who to trust, literally, with her life, and who she couldn't. She surrounded herself with wise counsel and those who brought her joy. Her choices were not random or impulsive. Rather, Elizabeth's choice to *aim high* assured the future she wanted to live. In today's world, as in the world you enter every time you leave your front door, to ensure the life and love you want, you need that same focused commitment to your greatest good. Your happiness depends on the wisdom, compassion and joy of the people you invite into your life. Enlightening your choices is the purpose of the next four chapters as we sink into the shadow side of intimate relationships.

Unfortunately, so many of our sisterhood are all too familiar with these cautionary tales. For those of you rare ones who aren't, through these stories you will understand what and who you may be inviting into your now-empowered life when you compromise yourself as you search for your Prince Charming. There are serious repercussions when you choose to love a broken man. However, if you choose wisely and without compromise ~ as Elizabeth ~ you will stand as a woman for what you believe in, for what you want, and for what you are worth.

JOURNEY JOURNALING:

If I choose mediocrity, what features of my slipper does this man not provide?

Realizing that his slipper will not fit comfortably, what discomfort am I willing to accept?

What is my true reason for the choice I make?

What level of honesty will I provide to Mr. Right Now?

What am I hoping to achieve by dating him?

What emotions come up when considering compromising my authenticity and/or my values just to have a man in my life?

RECOMMENDED READS:

Elizabeth: The Struggle for the Throne by David Starkey

Elizabeth I CEO: Strategic Lessons from the Leader who Built an Empire by Alan Axelrod

Watch Me Fly: What I Learned on the Way to Becoming the Woman I was Meant to Be by Myrlie Evers-Williams

17 Mr. Right vs. Mr. I'll Be Right Back:
The Joy of Commitment ~ Phobia

Wanted: Meaningful overnight relationship.

Personals Ad

Many women have loved a man who cannot love back. To put it simply, he's not just doing this to you. He's done it to every woman he's ever been involved with.

Steven Carter

Our Terms:

COMMITMENT: To pledge, promise, or engage oneself in a sincere involvement.

PHOBIA: Persistent, irrational fear or dread of a specific object, activity, or situation that leads to a compelling desire to avoid it.

You finally find your Mr. Right. He loves you like you've always dreamed. He says the right words, does all the right things, and promises you *Happily ever after*. Then, he begins to leave you.

You swallow your pride and promise him more than he ever promised you, so he will stay. You begin to question your sanity for what was once white is black; what was once true is false; what was once Mr. Right is now Mr. Wrong. Once you begin your long journey back to reality, you feel the gnawing fear that you may never trust the words *I love you* ever again.

MICHAEL

Michael's first memory of his mother was playing at her knee as she worked on her sewing machine in their small kitchen. As an adult, Michael's unconscious mind still holds his little boy sobs, pleas and tantrums that were never enough to attract his mother's attention away from her work and towards him. To survive his despair, he learned to be a child comfortable with distance. This child remains, hiding deep in Michael's mind. Today, Michael is a handsome, charming and success-ful banker who drives women to the brink. He is unaware that he has a problem, much less that his childhood trauma set him up to fear what he craves most: authentic emotional intimacy with a woman.

Michael *appears* to be a man on a quest for love. He dates often, and wines and dines women like a pro. He brings flowers on a first date, cries like a baby on the second, and melts hearts with *I love you* on the third. He knows what to say to make sure the woman feels safe. In between dates are endless calls, texts and tweets that are coming so fast and furiously that they border on obsessive-compulsive behavior. Michael is a master of seduction as he leads each chosen woman out of her common sense reality into his faux fantasy land. Her reluctance interests him. Her resistance intrigues him. *GAME ON!*

Michael professes that he wants to marry. To prove it, he's been engaged three times, once coming frighteningly close to the wedding day. He told his future bride the devastating news that he didn't love her anymore a whole 36 hours before he was to promise *Til death do us part*. In Michael's mind this was only fair.

Despite all appearances to the contrary, Michael's mission is not love, but conquest. He rushes into relationships with such vigor that women find it hard not to believe him, much less to resist him. But the moment they believe his words of love, and let their heart begin to dream of forever, he is saddling up his white steed, ready to bolt from the confinement of the castle walls.

All that these rejected women know is that Michael suddenly doesn't call when he says he will. He doesn't arrive when he says he will. He begins to find fault with them. He begins to avoid them. They are, of course, kept in the dark as to what has happened, or why. The same man who last week swore he could not live without them now either makes excuses to stay away, or just stays away without benefit of an excuse.

> **The one who cares the least controls the most.**
> Anonymous

As explained in Chapter 13, our earliest emotions were ruled by only one thing: the instinctual desperation to survive. When a young child is soothed by consistently safe and secure bonding with his parents, bliss happens. However, the indescribable emotional trauma of being a rejected, emotionally abandoned child detours nature's plan away from future healthy adult bonding, and towards a life-long, fear-based need to avoid enduring such pain ever again. That is why commitment-phobia defies all sense of logic ~ because it was birthed in early childhood, which is not a time of logic, but of feelings.

For a commitment-phobic male, early maternal rejection holds him captive to the paradox of craving what he fears most: love and connection. This includes Michael, who addictively runs towards love, but when love runs towards him the unconscious memory of his mother's refusal to nurture him overrides nature. So, his commitment-phobic cycle continues unabated and with gusto. As the hopes of each mystified woman are crushed by his irrational reversal, Michael remains clueless and detached.

He doesn't intentionally set out to hurt women. He truly wants intimacy. His very DNA wants intimacy. But, as he watches his current frustrated lover express her disbelief and emotional pain over his betrayal, Michael's limbic brain feels, like it was yesterday, the terror of his rejecting mother. Unknowingly, his newest ex-lover has innocently and tragically triggered his childhood pain, and he responds by pulling his emotional trigger on her.

Little Michael once had little choice but to seek comfort in his own inner world. Since he learned as a child to be comfortable with distance, by the time he was an adult he found normal physical and emotional intimacy threatening. Now, not just Michael, but his brain cannot link the pain he causes women to the pain from his mother's lack of nurturing. But his ritual of first winning, then rejecting the current *mother* figure ensures he wins his ultimate game of *gotcha!* Each woman, in her turn, becomes the powerless, pleading child begging for his affection, while he, the grownup, holds the power to reject her. As he once begged, the woman now begs. And that's how that plays out in the faux romance with any Mr. I'll Be Right Back.

Game Over. Start a New Game.

When attempting to dance with a commitment-phobic man, plan on having no plan except his plan. At first glance, you will notice him rushing towards you across the dance floor as if his very life depended on you extending your hand and simply uttering a grateful *yes.* You, on the other hand, are not so sure. This is how your dance begins. This is not how your dance will end. Although he will initially give all evidence to the contrary, the commitment-phobic man avoids intimacy because he finds it difficult, dare we say *impossible* to:

- Trust

- Become dependent on a woman

- Tolerate romantic partners who, quite naturally, want intimacy

Commitment-phobic men run the gamut of being somewhat uncomfortable to bolting like the runaway bride, but every single one of them exploits the trust of the women they woo.

Tell-Tale Signs You are Being Pursued
by a Commitment-Phobic Man

Before the 1ˢᵗ Date:

You may not find him that attractive, interesting and/or irresistible.

The more you appear reluctant, the more intense his pursuit.

On the 1st Date:

He is charming, attentive, sensitive, witty, generous, protective: i.e. *Perfect*

He makes you feel beautiful, special, intelligent, irresistible, safe: i.e. *Perfect*

You learn he has a history of failed relationships that he may, or may not, rationalize were not his fault.

After the 1ˢᵗ Date:

He sets up constant contact through emails, texts, tweets, phone calls, flower deliveries, greeting cards, and showing up *just to surprise you.*

He is comfortable with emotions, including crying about his childhood issues and past relationships.

He may profess to have a close relationship with his mother.

Before you are expecting it, he hints about making an exclusive commitment to you.

You test him and he passes. Examples: He helps you clean your windows; gives up his *boys' night out;* picks up your mom at the airport; holds you after sex...all night; fixes you breakfast the morning after; tells you you're beautiful when you look awful; kisses the tears from your cheeks.

He easily talks of a future together, including tomorrow, next week, next year and forever.

He says he wants children, or wishes you had been the mother of his children.

You have never felt so unconditionally loved and emotionally connected to a man.

He is everything you've ever dreamed of.

After the Last Date:

Coming full circle, how our chapter began is how our chapter ends: you finally found your Mr. Right. He loves you like you've always dreamed. He says the right words, does all the right things and promises you *happily ever after*. Then, he begins to leave you.

You swallow your pride and promise him more than he ever promised you, so he will stay. You begin to question your sanity, for what was once white is black; what was once true is false; what was once Mr. Right is Mr. Oh So Very, Very Wrong! Then, once you begin your long journey back to reality, you feel the gnawing fear that you may never trust the words *I love you* again.

Note:

He may not find his next *victim* right away, so he calls, repenting of his sin of abandoning you. If you take his bait, he will cycle through any or all of the above in much less time that your first time around. Or, he will repeat any or all of the above with the next woman to replace you. The hidden dynamic for Mr. I'll be Right Back, whether with you or with a new victim, will be to ensure that he always maintains the power and control in the relationship.

The phrase *If it looks too good to be true, it probably is* was never truer then when you are the prey of a commitment-phobic man. The great news is that now, as *NaughtABimbeaux*, your desperation has evolved to Dignity. You can spot a commitment-phobe a mile away.

Be prepared, however. He who woos and wins every woman he wants will simply not understand how his irresistible charm and flattery cannot get him to 1st base, much less a 1st date, with you. For a man like Michael, your absolute resistance shifts his *Game On* to THE OLYMPIC GAMES!

As a woman like Elizabeth I of England, you stand. And as you so elegantly bid him farewell, he will not hear your deep sigh of relief as you remember how desperately you once believed such a man's promises were true; how you invented all sorts of ridiculous reasons why he turned away; how you willingly begged for his love, as your denial of the obvious bled your self-worth dry.

How You Untangled Your Heart from His Web of Lies

1. Opened your tear-filled eyes.

2. Saw the episode as abuse of your trust and affection.

3. Totally disengaged from any and all contact.

4. Moved through paralyzing grief to empowering rage.

5. Determined you would not waste your suffering.

6. Chose to be *NaughtABimbeaux*.

7. Shifted *Will he like me?* to **Is he WORTHY of Me?**

You are the only one responsible for protecting your self-worth. You are the only one who can make a vow to your own emotional well-being ~ first, last and always. That promise guarantees you will stay safe, focused, and nurtured while you walk step-by-step on the path that leads to the rest of your life.

JOURNEY JOURNALING:

How does this information clarify why some men are afraid of a relationship?

What men have I dated who were commitment-phobic?

What were their first clues that I ignored or excused?

What specific actions will I take to avoid another commitment-phobic relationship?

RECOMMENDED READS:

Men Who Can't Love: How To Recognize a Commitmentphobic Man Before He Breaks Your Heart by Steven Carter and Julia Sokol

Women Who Love Too Much: When You Keep Wishing and Hoping He'll Change by Robin Norwood

The Little Black Book of Big Red Flags: Relationship Warning Signs You Totally Spotted...But Chose to Ignore by Natasha Burton, Julie Fishman and Meagan McCrary

18 *Mr. Right vs. Mr. Always Right:*
The Joy of Narcissism, aka 'King Me'

He was like a cock who thought the sun had risen to hear him crow.
George Eliot

Women know how to fake orgasm. Men know how to fake an entire relationship.
Sharon Stone

You're so vain. You probably think this song is about you.
Carly Simon

Our Terms:

NARCISSIST: Person with excessive pride or obsession with one's own appearance, qualities, achievements; inordinate fascination with self, excessive self-love; feels entitled; vain.

SOCIOPATH: Person without a sense of moral or social conscience; disregard for the effects of behavior on others; willing to lie, steal, violate, betray, con, or charm others to achieve personal goals; loves things, uses people.

CONTROL: The act of exercising power over oneself or others; to dominate, regulate or command.

EXPLOIT: To take advantage of; to use selfishly for one's own ends; to manipulate another person for one's own advantage.

INTIMACY: A state of close, personal, affectionate, respectful relationship; arising from familiar experience, security and connection; pertaining to the innermost private or essential nature.

CINDY

Cindy had passed her state's real estate license exam and was hired by a firm known for its friendly sales force. She'd been working there about a week when one of the married realtors, Melinda, mentioned she had a new client, a *new man in town*, who was handsome, wealthy, and single. Steve had noticed Cindy's photo in the Realtor's Gallery, and commented to Melinda how beautiful she was, and then asked if she was available. Melinda called Cindy on her cell and asked if it would be OK if she gave Steve her number. Cindy's heart fluttered a bit as she told Melinda, *Sure.*

The very next evening, Steve called and within minutes asked her to dinner on Friday night. With a full life building her new business, working out, and socializing with her friends, Cindy responded, *I'd love to. I'll run get my calendar to double-check; be back in a second.* In less than a minute our ingénue had checked her calendar and confirmed with Steve that Friday night would be perfect. Since he was new in town, he asked if she had a favorite restaurant. Cindy suggested a lovely European Café near her office. *Fine, I'll meet you there at 7:00.*

The week was busy with showing property to new clients, but hidden under her calm demeanor Cindy sensed the hopeful thrill of anticipation. She arrived at the small cafe, fashionably late at ten minutes passed seven. Surely, Steve would have arrived by now, eagerly waiting to finally meet her. Her tummy tightened underneath her new dress as she scanned the small room and saw only couples. The Maître D seated her facing the door. Cindy innocently waited for this man for over an hour; this man who had decided ~ firmly decided one week before, as they arranged the time and place of their dinner date ~ that if she needed to check her calendar before committing to meet him, she was not a woman deserving of his time.

> **A thousand half-loves must be forsaken**
> **to take one whole heart home.**
> Rumi

Nobody can be kinder than the narcissist while you react to life on his own terms.
Elizabeth Bowen

To accommodate his fragile ego, every situation, every dilemma for the narcissist begins and ends with power and control. Having never matured from the infantile, ego-centric *I* to the relationship-oriented *I & Thou*, he makes very sure that he alone is the Star of his one-man play ~ *The Life of Me*. If he decides to invite you onto his stage, remember your role will be as a prop that supports his self-expression. You need only to read from his script and follow his direction without question. Never forget that there is only one star on the stage of his life, and make no mistake, it isn't you. Your only value is to make sure you read your lines exactly as he writes them, and act out, flawlessly, his direction. Cast in a supporting role, you will never experience how the spotlight feels on your face.

Cindy spent one evening disappointed and dining alone, stood up by a narcissist. Alison was not so lucky.

ALISON

One memory for Alison stands out now that she's escaped. It happened the night her boyfriend, Dick, rented a movie depicting an abused woman terrorized by her husband. Alison, knowing she had to choose her words carefully to avoid another argument, told him she was going to bed early because the movie upset her.

Just one year before, Alison was flattered by Dick's obvious attention when they met at a friend's party. He was easy to talk to, they were both marathon runners, and those eyes of his went straight to her soul. Soon, they were dating exclusively, and Alison's iPhone overflowed with Dick's *love notes*. He always expected her to respond immediately, but sometimes her work schedule got in the way. Alison knew his next tweets would be more scolding than loving.

Alison enjoyed his attention, even though it was a bit intrusive at times. She'd never had such an attentive boyfriend. In time, she felt sure they could share a wonderful life, so when he asked her, she moved into his home up in the hills above the city. That was when the other side of Dick broke through. One night after discussing politics, Dick threw her into the wall. Alison was stunned but assured him she'd be fine by morning. When it happened again two weeks later, Alison started packing.

> *The first time a woman is hit, she is a victim.*
> *The second time, she is a volunteer.*
> *Thousands of cases have made it clear to me*
> *that getting away safely is wiser than trying*
> *to change the abusive husband.*
> Gavin DeBecker

At her office the next day, flowers arrived, and then more flowers arrived, this time with a huge balloon that said *I'm sorry*. When she got home, Dick had cooked a gourmet dinner and poured her a glass of her favorite Cabernet. Then, he put down his glass, took her face in his hands and said the words her soul longed to hear him say, *Alison, I don't know what came over me. I promise you, I will never hurt you again.* Alison believed him. After all, they loved each other.

Dick kept that promise until the second day of their honeymoon, two years later. From then on, it seemed to Alison like the violence never stopped. Dick had always been a teaser, but now the teasing had an edge, an edge aimed right at her. But the teasing was the least of it. She was hiding bruises and split lips under her makeup. That wasn't the only makeup she was using to hide reality. She was making-up excuses to her concerned coworkers, friends and family.

> *Emotional abuse almost always escalates to physical violence.*
> Diane Lass, Ph.D., Family Justice Center, San Diego

Dick blamed his *bouts* on stress at work and financial pressures. But Alison knew that other partners faced the same issues, yet their wives weren't being berated, beaten and choked. In the beginning, Alison blamed herself. Dick treated her like a queen before they married. What was she doing now that made him so angry? She tried to build him up, but the more she tried the more he tore her down. It seemed that she couldn't figure out what set him off. Her friends asked her, *How can you possibly predict his triggers? You're not a psychic.* But, Alison didn't listen.

Instead, she tried harder to be the perfect wife. Sometimes, she actually felt it worked. Dick would be his sweet self, like she remembered. They would have friends over for barbeques in their backyard, and everyone would laugh and have a great evening. Alison's heart would tell her *It's OK, now. Everything is going to be fine.* It was during one of those sweet times that Alison got pregnant. Then, Dick's battering took aim at their unborn baby. Alison didn't want her marriage to end, just the kicking of her belly. She pleaded to protect their child. She fantasized that Dick would fall in love with this baby and would be the perfect husband and father.

But the baby was colicky. Before stomping out of the nursery at 2 AM, Dick would scream at her and his newborn son. When their baby's colic continued for weeks on end, Dick's yelling escalated, and before long both Alison and her baby were being hit. The next day, Alison would threaten to leave. Dick would, predictably, become remorseful and promising her through his tears *I'm so sorry, please please don't' go. I promise I will never hurt you again.* That became their dance, or what therapists call *The Cycle of Violence.*

Alison could always tell when Dick's rage was about to strike. She could see it in his eyes. On that final day, while Dick sat in his downtown office unaware, Alison, walking on egg shells, held their baby in her arms and walked out their front door, forever.

The scientific community notes a well-established psychological difference between males and females. Males' predominant hormone, testosterone, fuels their aggressive tendencies. When used for good, their aggression protects their families from harm. But when this natural protective instinct is undermined by emotional vulnerability from childhood, rather than protecting, loved ones become their targets. The male's tendency towards violence is one of the best established and most pervasive of all psychological gender differences.

One in twenty-five everyday Americans is secretly a sociopath.
They could be your colleague, your neighbor, even family, and they
can do literally anything at all and feel absolutely no guilt.
Martha Stout, Ph.D., Harvard Psychologist,
The Sociopath Next Door

According to a *Domestic Violence* study by the Centers for Disease Control and Prevention:

60% of Women have Experienced Abuse

- 62% have been hit, shoved, or slapped
- 33% have been choked or strangled
- 11%, who say their partner is currently abusive, predict he will seriously hurt or kill them
- 23% admit they suffered physical violence, such as being slapped or punched.
- 94% cite emotional abuse.

Women Keep Quiet about Their Abuse

- 24% of women in abusive relationships have not told anyone they're being harmed.
- 37% of women who have known someone in such a relationship never said anything to that person or to the authorities.

Note: I highly recommend the following link for comprehensive information on date rape, domestic violence, and how to recognize signs of an abusive personality.

http://www.datehookup.com/content-abuse-advice-an-online-resource-guide-on-domestic-violence.htm

The bimbo believes the power of love overcomes the love of power.
'Don't count on it,' answers the wise NaughtABimbeaux.
Morgan Rose

Broken Men Come in Every Race, Class and Religion

Alison and Cindy's stories show how a relationship with a Mr. Always Right can run the gamut from the narcissistic *close call* to the sociopathic *run for your life.* Unfortunately, such men can be found in every level of society. They often seek power positions such as CEO, therapist, director, physician, professor, pastor, lawyer, teacher, coach, or politician. Any career that offers power, control and influence will attract Mr. Always Right. How convenient for him that appearing powerful also attracts innocent, emotionally insecure women who seek such a man as he appears to be. That's why, when needing a power fix, Mr. Always Right hunts for the vulnerable woman, a woman naïve enough to be lured in by his flattering lies.

For instance, if you appear unsure, shy, or helpless he will shape-shift into whatever man he thinks you are looking for. If you are lonely and needy, he will make you feel special and important. If you have low self-esteem, he will tell you you're beautiful, talented, and wise. If you have doubts about him, he will win your sympathy and devotion. If you resist, he will become irresistible. He will convince you that every other woman has betrayed him, but you are the only one who has ever truly understood him, and therefore the *only* woman he can trust.

All of the above characteristics apply to both the narcissist and the sociopath. And, as reflected in our stories, though the narcissist may have fewer tendencies towards overt pathology, neither of them have a conscience. Once they take from you what they need and move on, you can be sure they won't bother turning around to see the chaos they have left behind in their wake, also known as *your life*.

The signature difference between them is that the narcissist may break your heart; the sociopath will break your heart, your bones, even your life.

Meet Dr. JEKYLL & Mr. HYDE

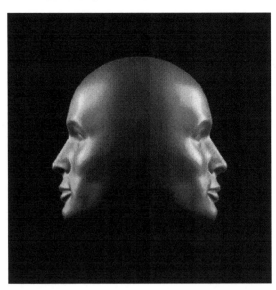

By analyzing all available records on hundreds of cases,
I have come to see that Scott Peterson and other serial killers do not
kill for the reasons normally ascribed to spousal murderers.

They eliminate the women, and sometimes children, in their lives
because they no longer serve any useful purpose to them. They view
those they once claimed to love as inconveniences, impediments to
the kind of life they covet and fantasize for themselves.
Marilee Strong, Why Scott Peterson is a Narcissist

When you know what to look for, a sociopath is not hard to spot. To attract the attention he craves he can be energetic, charismatic, charming and witty. In reality he is a master manipulator who lies, deceives, stalks, steals and commits fraud. In the initial courtship, he will appear compassionate, but he is not. Once he has sucked you into his world, charming Dr. Jekyll soon reveals his true identity: ruthless, pathological Mr. Hyde.

The sociopath is a predator. Like a vampire sucking blood to survive, he needs a vulnerable woman to maintain his fix of power and control. If you've been with such a man you know the drill. Try to figure out his triggers, and he'll come up with new ones. Try to debate, argue, or convince him of any reasonable point, and you will be flooded with double talk. If you continue to question or confront him, you quickly learn that compromise is not in his vocabulary. Winning the power struggle is how he defines intimacy. To prove it, he will punish you if he perceives you are a threat to his power. He can become violent and his rage targets those he claims to love. Yes, even children. It's not uncommon that while he shows no mercy to you, he's already charming your replacement as if you never existed.

You are not, nor ever will be, a person to love. Neither is he, nor ever will be, a person who loves any other human but himself. Beneath the perfect image he projects to the world lurks a self-centered, ego-driven, cruel mind that targets one goal with laser focus ~ to take and keep ownership of your life. Once he knows that you believe his lies, like a modern day *Phantom of the Opera*, he will drag you ~ heart, body and soul ~ deeper and deeper into his pit of hell.

One has to wonder how such rigidity and rage can develop within the soul of a man. Do such characteristics just appear out of a vacuum? Out of a peaceful life does violence just suddenly explode? A growing field of research tells us that such severe ego-centric pathology often is birthed in one's earliest days when innocence was as fragile as a baby's tears.

Who are the BONOBOS &
Why are We Talking about Them Now?

Bonobo apes are the most gentle of creatures, unique among primates in their high intelligence, emotional awareness, and compassion. They actually look and act more like humans than other apes. This is probably because **bonobos share over 98 % of our human DNA.** Because they are our closest cousins, anthropologists have studied them for decades. One of their most important findings: mommy bonobo holds onto her sons twice as long as her daughters. Long after baby girl has moved on, baby boy bonobo is still attached like Velcro to his mommy.

These creatures are a lot like our babies in this way. When mommy isn't within sight, mommy doesn't exist. And, if mommy doesn't exist, baby's survival fear kicks in. Literally holding on to her fur satisfies his little ape brain's desperation that mommy isn't going anywhere without him. And, to make absolutely sure he completes this crucial primary developmental stage, mommy bonobo will not conceive her next child until her baby boy decides he's ready to run free on his own.

When researchers separate a mother and son before he's emotionally ready to detach, baby boy bonobo goes on tilt, as in crashes into a mental meltdown from the terror of losing his life line. Now that his brain has felt fear he will never recover his innate traits of peace, playfulness, and innocence. Rather, his primal fear of threatened extinction emerges as uncharacteristic rage. If returned to his peaceful colony, he will terrorize it. You would think that bonobo females wouldn't touch him with a ten foot pole...ever. In fact, if a girl bonobo could talk, she'd probably describe him with words like *sociopathic* and *rageaholic*. If he tries to come near her, rather than run from him in fear, our courageous primate female cousin runs towards him and rips off his testicles! That's what our bonobo sisters call *keeping the peace*.

Given that we and the bonobos are practically identical DNA twins, could this research ~ focused on the profound importance of mother/ infant son bonding ~ provide clues as to why our society increasingly confronts escalating pathology, violence, and random acts of terror, specifically by our men and boys? Might it answer, also, why male violence most often targets women, the symbol of their *mother rage*?

We are All Born Ego-Centric

Human babies are born into the world of *I*. Our little baby brain has no way to understand who our parents are, where the milk comes from, or why we cry. We just know about *I*.

From birth through your 3rd birthday, your parents had a window of opportunity to nurture you so well that you began to notice *Hey! I'm not alone here. I've got creatures who feed me when I'm hungry, change me when I'm wet, giggle when I giggle, then rock me to sleep in their arms. This is pretty cool.* Their nurturing made you feel secure and happy. So, lo and behold, your little world of *I* began to expand to *I & Thou*. If they neglected your needs and cries, you didn't budge from your little world of *I* because it was just too scary out there.

Whether human or bonobo, it's not hard to see how critical the parent's role is for moving their child from *I* to *I & Thou.*

Said another way, parents hold the power to shift their child's personality from egotistical to empathetic by being consistently loving. Thus, consistent parental nurturing is required for raising a compassionate, humane adult. If we're talking about men (which we have been for a while here), like our bonobo boy cousins, if within the most primary relationship, mommy earned his trust, his brain learned it's safe to trust females. If she failed to earn his trust, his terror of abandonment froze his emotional development for adult attachment and intimacy. Clinicians refer to this pathology as *arrested development.*

Early childhood is the starting point for all love and for all cruelty in later years. To the degree that a child has been given compassion, they will pass it on to others in the future.
Alice Miller, Psychotherapist

We met Michael in our last chapter. His first memories are having to cry in his futile attempt to attract his mother's attention while she sewed on. She was physically and emotionally unavailable to fulfill the developmental needs of her young son. As a man, Michael's internal conflict manifests in his eagerness to be physically available to women while he withholds his emotional attachment, which remains stuck in his *I* of infancy. Michael is not physically dangerous, but he inflicts deep emotional pain through his addiction for winning, then rejecting women.

No matter the level of pathology, a broken man needs his addictions to numb the pain of innocence lost. He may be addicted to money, position, drugs, alcohol, pornography, gambling, or conquest. Whatever his *drug of choice,* his ultimate aim is to guarantee he holds absolute power and control. There is nothing a woman can do to change this. As long as a woman feeds a man's infantile ego, he will do whatever and say whatever he needs to ensure she stays to dance their codependent dance. Once she no longer serves his needs, he will loathe her, then leave her or worse.

Do not become a victim and the oppression will stop.
The Tao of Women

Warning:
The root of all domestic violence is narcissism. Children raised in fear-based environments absorb the narcissism of their parents, and are seriously at risk to repeat it. Narcissistic violence, on the continuum from verbal violence to physical assault, becomes the family legacy. If a woman trusts a Mr. Always Right, she dooms herself, and any children

she may have, to years, if not the rest of her life, to being emotionally, mentally, financially, physically and spiritually crippled. Until our families, communities, and nation seriously address and heal this malignancy, we will all suffer the consequences. And, have no doubt, it will be our children who pay the price.

> ***Deep inside us, we know what every family therapist knows:***
> ***the problems between the parents***
> ***become the problems within the children.***
> Roger Gould

What Takes Place in the World Starts in the Home

In the next chapter you will learn why males are more vulnerable than females in their physical, emotional, and relational response to fear-based childhoods. This information is critical to discerning frog from prince, for when you stand at the altar, there will be not two, but four of you. Each of you brings with you your inner child.

JOURNEY JOURNALING:

Who are the narcissistic men I have allowed to control me?

What narcissistic characteristics will I now recognize/avoid?

What narcissistic characteristics are attractive/repulsive to me?

RECOMMENDED READS:

The Sociopath Next Door: The Ruthless Versus the Rest of Us by Martha Stout

The Wizard of Oz and Other Narcissists: Coping with the One-Way Relationship in Work, Love, and Family by Eleanor Payson

Why is it Always About You?: The Seven Deadly Sins of Narcissism by Sandy Hotchkiss and James Masterson

Will I Ever Be Good Enough?: Healing the Daughters of Narcissistic Mothers by Karyl McBride

Children of the Self-Absorbed: A Grown-Up's Guide to Getting Over Narcissistic Parents by Nina Brown

Narcissistic Lovers: How to Cope, Recover and Move On by Cynthia Zane and Kevin Dibble

Freeing Yourself from the Narcissist in Your Life by Linda Martinez-Lewis

Why Does He Do That?: Inside the Minds of Angry and Controlling Men by Lundy Bancroft

Ghosts from the Nursery: Tracing the Roots of Violence by Robin Karr-Morse

'Ghosts from the Nursery' is used to express the idea that murderers, and other violent criminals, who were once infants in our communities, are always accompanied by the spirits of the babies they once were, together with the forces that killed their promise.
Robin Karr-Morse, Ghosts from the Nursery

- 1 out of 3 of America's daughters is sexually violated before age 18.

- 1 out of 5 of America's sons is sexually violated before age 18.

- More pregnant women are killed by the father of their unborn child than by accidents and illness combined.

- Men are the primary suspects when their own children, mothers, sisters, girlfriends and wives have been raped, kidnapped, mutilated, or killed.

In his book, *The Gift of Fear*, Gavin De Becker states that **every thirty seconds a woman is raped** in America. He goes on to say, *If a* *full jumbo jet crashed into a mountain killing everyone on board, and if that happened every month, month in and month out, the number of people killed still wouldn't equal the number of women murdered by their husbands and boyfriends each year.*

What is the ACE Study and Why Is It Important to Me?

The ACE Study is one of the largest scientific research studies of its kind, with over 17,000 middle income Americans participating. The focus was to analyze the relationship between **childhood trauma** and the risk for **physical and mental illness in adulthood**.

Over the course of a decade, the results demonstrated a strong, graded relationship between the level of traumatic stress in childhood and poor physical, mental and behavioral outcomes later in life.

What is an Adverse Childhood Experience (ACE)?

Growing up experiencing any of the following conditions in the household prior to age 18:

- Recurrent physical abuse
- Recurrent emotional abuse
- Contact sexual abuse
- An alcohol and/or drug abuser in the household
- An incarcerated household member
- Family member who is chronically depressed, mentally ill, institutionalized, or suicidal
- Mother is treated violently
- One or no parents
- Physical neglect
- Emotional neglect

How does FEAR Impact Childhood?

The key concept of the ACE Study is that stressful or traumatic childhood experiences can result in social, emotional, and cognitive impairments. Examples: Increased risk of unhealthy behaviors, risk of violence or re-victimization, disease, disability and *early death.*

Breakthroughs in neurobiology demonstrate that fear-based childhoods disrupt neurodevelopment and can actually alter normal brain structure and function.

Fear in infancy and early childhood has a cumulative impact on childhood development. Results of the ACE Study link the exploding rates in America's physical, mental, and social pathologies with our national failure to strengthen our families and protect our children.

A decade of rigorous research demonstrates that sustained stress in childhood results in overproduction of cortisols, with profound, lifelong impacts on the brain and body.

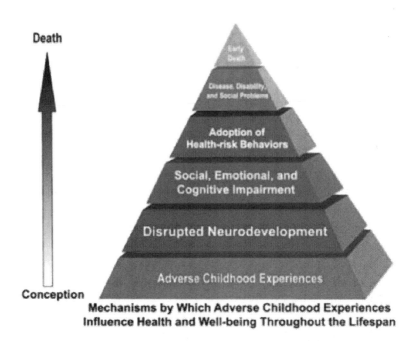

Mechanisms by Which Adverse Childhood Experiences Influence Health and Well-being Throughout the Lifespan

The ACE Score

The ACE Study used a simple scoring method to determine the extent of each study participant's exposure to childhood trauma. Exposure to one category (not incident) of ACE, qualifies as one point. When the points are added up, the ACE Score is determined. An ACE Score of 0 (zero) would mean that the person reported no exposure to any of the categories of trauma listed. An ACE Score of 10 would mean that the person reported exposure to all of the categories of trauma listed.

What is Your ACE Score?

Find out at http://www.AcesTooHigh.com

What Health Risks are Associated with ACEs?

The young brain is especially vulnerable to stress. When prolonged stress occurs during infancy and childhood, the hormone cortisol is released throughout the young brain and body. These stress hormones compromise normal brain development and the immature immune and nervous systems. The ACE Study demonstrates that early stress is a strong factor for developing the following national health pandemics:

- Cardiovascular disease
- Cancer
- Heart attacks
- High blood pressure
- Stroke
- Diabetes
- Weight gain (especially abdominal fat)
- Exhaustion
- Reduced Growth Hormone Levels
- Compromised immune function

How Does the ACE Score Effect Society?

Within the 17,000 middle-class, ethnically diverse American adults tested, it was found that the compulsive use of nicotine, alcohol, and injected street drugs increased proportionally, in a strong, graded, dose-response manner, with the level of adverse life experiences reported during childhood.

The ACE Study results are disturbing because they imply that the basic causes of addictions are found in our personal histories, not in drug dealers or dangerous chemicals. This finding is at odds with current concepts, including those of biological psychiatry, drug-treatment programs, and drug-eradication programs. The results of the ACE Study strongly suggest that billions of dollars are spent everywhere except on the solution.

The prevalence of ACEs and their long-term effects are a major determinant of the health and social well-being of the nation. This is true whether from the standpoint of social costs, the economics of health care, the quality of human existence, the focus of medical treatment, or the effects of public policy.

The ACE Study demonstrates dramatically that if citizens engage in the protection and nurturing of all children, these serious and prevalent health and social problems will be significantly reduced.

Where can I Find More Information on the ACE Study?

http://www.acestudy.org/

http://www.cdc.gov/ace/index.htm

http://acestoohigh.com/about/

Full downloadable PDF articles on Major ACE Study Findings:http://www.annafoundation.org/ACE%20STUDY%20FINDINGS.html

The ACE Study is an ongoing collaboration between the Centers for Disease Control and Prevention and Kaiser Permanente.

19 *Little Boy Blue:*
The Vulnerability of Grownup Little Boys

It is easier to build strong children
than to repair broken men.
Frederick Douglass

Normal affect development does not occur when the parents
are unable to read the emotional cues of their infant.
Taylor, Bagby, and Parker, *Disorders of Affect Regulation*

On and on the rain will fall like tears from a star,
like tears from a star. On and on the rain will say
how fragile we are, how fragile we are.
Sting

Our Terms:

VULNERABLE: Susceptible to being wounded, physically or emotionally; defenseless against criticism or moral attack; open to assault; difficult to defend.

FRAGILE: Easily broken, shattered, damaged or destroyed; delicate; brittle; unstable; precarious; vulnerable; lacking physical or emotional strength.

ABANDON: To leave completely and finally forsake; withdraw from; desert; banish.

Seems like whenever women gather these days, the conversation eventually gets around to *Where have all the good men gone?* By good, we mean men who are honest, intelligent, and financially and emotionally stable. Most importantly, we mean men capable of sharing a conscious, emotionally intimate relationship with similarly inclined women.

As Chapter 18 explained, our closest cousins, the bonobo apes, do this very well in their little ape way…so well, in fact, that they are one of the most peaceful, secure, and emotionally healthy cultures on our planet.

However, there is one glaring difference between baby boy bonobo and baby boy human. When baby boy bonobo can't find his mommy, he takes about a nanosecond to shoot from 0 to 60 on the rage scale. But the path to pathology for the emotionally abandoned human male can take years as he struggles from infancy to adulthood through rather predictable stages.

Clinicians have observed that men with pathological tendencies often share a specific characteristic profile.

Temperament, Intellect and Childhood Dynamics of Emotionally Detached, Potentially Dangerous Men:

- Higher than average cognitive and/or emotional I.Q.
- Early indications of heightened emotional sensitivity, including empathy for animals and children.
- Early indications of a mature understanding and/or emotional intensity around issues of justice, fairness, and kindness.
- Artistic curiosity, appreciation, and abilities, including music, art, poetry, literature.
- Rigid, authoritarian, rejecting and/or inconsistent parenting.
- Traumatized and/or unpredictable early home environment.

Temperament + Intelligence + Poor Parenting = Narcissistic / Commitmentphobic / Rageaholic Traits

The Unnatural Development of the
Emotionally Abandoned Male

The greatest terror a child can have is that he is not loved,
and rejection is the hell he fears. I think everyone in the world,
to a large or small extent, has felt rejection. And with rejection
comes anger, and with anger some kind of crime in revenge for the
rejection, and with the crime guilt, and there is the story of mankind.
John Steinbeck

Mental health research demonstrates that people capable and eager for emotional commitment are most often the products of emotionally healthy parents who were committed to meeting the emotional needs of their children. The following describes how the opposite happens.

How to Create a Broken Male Child

1st Stage: DESPERATION ~ Newborn through Toddlerhood

Parents have no idea what temperament or intelligence their little newborn bundle brings into their home. But no matter the temperament or intelligence, every baby has one primary need ~ *Survival.* And one surefire way to meet it ~ CRY! When the distress signal sounds, conscious human parents do what bonobo parents do. They respect the needs of their child and so soothe his distress. Typically, brighter than average babies are *difficult* babies, as in demanding, easily bored and *high strung.* That's often the first clue that this baby's brain has a high awareness of his environment and how well his needs are being met. When parents nurture these needs, baby learns he can trust his parents to meet them. Love is good for this happy baby.

But when the highly aware baby's cries are punished or ignored, he tries harder. After all, his cries signal **HELP!** If his parents do not rescue him, he just screams louder and longer. He can't give up because his terror of dying triggers his brain's *fight or flight* response, of which he can do neither. *Alert, aware babies have been known to sob desperately for an hour or more.* At some point, mommy or daddy may punish these *tantrums* by denying him attention even more than they already do. To punish his *neediness,* they may give him a *time out.* After all, baby needs to learn who's in charge in this family! Of course, Junior may be brighter than the average baby, but he still has no ability to understand such concepts as power, control and abandonment. He just knows how to cry to survive if he has to. With repeated episodes, his terror releases stress hormones that specifically target his limbic brain's amygdala and hippocampus, the areas of emotional regulation and memory. His parents' failure to comfort him destroys vital opportunities to develop trust, security and empathy between them and their baby. These early traumatic episodes compromise his brain's later adult emotional functioning. For this innocent desperate baby, love is not so good.

2ⁿᵈ Stage: DISSILUSIONMENT ~ Approximate ages 2 – 10

Junior is evolving into Little Boy Blue. Just as he did in infancy, he clings to the hope that he can figure out what he has to do to attract his parents' attention and affection. Unfortunately, he's now old enough to figure out that what he's doing isn't working. So, he tries to become *good,* or at least good enough to win their approval to ensure his survival. For instance, when he learns a new skill, like riding his two wheeler or building the tallest block tower ever, he looks for their approval: *Mommy! Look! Daddy, watch me!* When that doesn't work, he falls back on the tantrum approach. It hasn't worked that well for him in the past, but maybe this time *mommy* or *daddy* might decide to notice him.

Even though he's an intelligent child, his parents' message, *I love you as long as you are the child I want you to be,* is way beyond what his above average brain can understand. So, if being *good* wasn't good enough, rather than give up, he will earnestly try to become the perfect child, as in adorable, helpful, and irresistible. But around the age of seven or eight he will realize that all of his desperate attempts to win his parents' attention, much less their approval, have been futile. They are just too busy, disinterested, angry or absent to notice him, to care for him. About this time is when he will begin to give up hope.

Self-portraits: "This is me in a box suffering," and "That's me," by Christopher, a 7-year-old "emotionally abandoned" little boy.

Men do not become what, by nature, they are meant to be, but what society makes them. Generous feelings are, as it were, shrunk up, seared, violently wrenched, and amputated to fit us for our intercourse with the world, something in the manner that beggars maim and mutilate their children to make them fit for their future situation in life.

E. Colby

3rd Stage: ADOLESCENT / TEEN PATHOLOGY
Approximate ages 10 – 21

The emptiness from Little Boy Blue's childhood now collides with adolescence. Both his defense mechanisms and male hormones are thrusting him forward into the new-found power of his teenage years. He may try to prove his parents wrong by becoming a top student, athlete, or campus leader. Or, he may try to prove them right by self-sabotaging his grades, health, reputation, and opportunities for the future.

Given time, he hopes being good enough, smart enough, clever enough, fast enough, or handsome enough will attract the attention of an adult parent-replacement figure. So, he looks past his parent to find a teacher, coach, clergy, or extended family member. If he teams with a healthy adult who is genuinely supportive, his wounded ego may relearn love, albeit second hand. If targeted by a predator who has purposefully chosen his career field to abuse children, Little Boy Blue's fragile ego will make him easy prey. If he can find no one, emotionally healthy or not, having exhausted all options for finding someone who thinks he has value (i.e., who thinks he is worthy of love), his self-worth is swallowed up by the totality of the world's rejection. Finding no one to love him as he is, he fights back with his first authentically serious episodes of passive aggressiveness, violation, depression and/or overt rage.

For a kid seething with *mother rage*, teenage romance weaves a treacherous web of hope and fear as he drags all the baggage from his baby days on his quest to find it. His insecure attempts to appear secure with girls mask his maternally-deprived fear of being rejected, again. He is clueless how love reciprocates between partners. He has no such emotional template to draw from. He's just a stranger in a strange land, trying to look cool. Even though he is desperate to fill the void in his heart, he will sabotage relationships he so desperately wants and needs. And, his teenage mind fills with fear.

The Child is the Father of the Man
William Wordsworth

4ᵗʰ Stage: ADULT PATHOLOGY

As an adult, Little Boy Blue's childhood hopelessness returns, recycling the pain of his infancy into narcissistic rigidity that will poison his own marriage and parenting. His rage masks his intense fear of intimacy, and his shame for failing to be *perfect*. His *bravado* masks his intense fear of being rejected. His grownup, closed-down mind works overtime to stuff down years of feeling afraid no one will ever love him because he is unlovable.

Romantically, nothing has changed since his teen years. For each grown up Little Boy Blue, love with a woman still weaves a treacherous, terrifying web of hope and fear. He's still just a stranger in a strange land. He remains clueless how love reciprocates between partners, having no such emotional template to draw from. He wrestles with the paradox of wanting a woman, yet in his unconscious mind every woman represents *mommy,* the target of his *mother rage.* So he marries. He divorces. He fathers children. He has affairs. He leaves a trail of broken promises and broken hearts. He deceives and tries too hard. He grabs at power and demands control. He withholds affection to punish those who should know better.

He blames every woman who *fails* him for the sins of his mother. Whatever else goes wrong he blames on those around him, those he says he loves. He can't blame himself because he's tried being good enough, smart enough, clever enough, rich enough, and handsome enough. Of course, doesn't he know by now that none of it will ever be enough? Doesn't he realize how he has recycled his childhood pain into his wife, children, and lovers? Will he ever have the emotional strength to admit that his greatest success was in passing on his family legacy of pain, rejection and loneliness?

Rejected by his parents, girlfriends, lovers and wives, and possibly his children, he retreats even further into the familiar, into the Great Narcissistic *I* of infancy. A lonely, tormented man, his whole being still cries out for love like the sweet baby he once was. His paralyzing loneliness forces him to try, yet again, to hunt down the love that so far eludes him, the life-saving love that will fix all that is broken within him. His primal fear ignites that frantic moment of survival panic when he ventures out from the dark night of his soul, desperately looking for women online, or in line, or anywhere else there's a chance to meet **you**.

We're only just now beginning to understand the underlying weakness of men, for so many centuries almost universally projected onto women.
Sebastian Kraemer, Ph.D.

Before your journey to becoming *NaughtABimbeaux*, you had very few clues to make sense of the nonsense that so often detoured your search for that one wonderful man able to love you. Having read the past four chapters, you are likely filled with fear **big time**! Not only fear for your safety, but also fear that, with so few emotionally healthy men available, your hopes for happiness are doomed...

Where, oh where, can your Prince be?

You are certainly normal to wonder how you can ever find an honest, intelligent, financially and emotionally stable man capable of sharing a conscious emotionally intimate relationship. Surely all the good men are either happily married, gay, extinct, or at least on the endangered species list. There are probably more healthy bonobo males than human males!

Kissing a Frog into a Prince Only Works in Fairy Tales

Since you probably prefer a human male to an ape, and you're about to press the PANIC BUTTON in your heart, does all this talk about broken baby boys have the potential to catapult you right back to Bimboland? Are you hearing that small voice of days gone by reminding you that you are a warm, forgiving, full-to-the-brim with compassion *Ms. Empathy Queen*? I mean, after all, you are a woman looking to love a man, and not just any woman, but a *NaughtABimbeaux*. So, if you can't find your prince, maybe you can fix a frog. This may sound reasonable now that you know the dance. Certainly, with a little patience, you can teach him the steps. Right? **WRONG!!!!** As *NaughtABimbeaux*, you recognize that your power does not include the power to change him. **You hold the power to change just one person, and you have taken it**. He has the same choice to change, and only he can choose it.

The good news is that unlike wounded bonobos, some wounded human males have eventually recognized that all of the negativity and terror of their early lives could not destroy their true goodness. Many have courageously placed their childhood pain into the hands of a trained, compassionate therapist who skillfully unraveled all the knots, then supported life anew for these grown up, reborn Little Boy Blues.

These special men willingly trek back into their most primal pain, like a baby crawling terrified through a mine field of memories and emotions. Watching their rebirth reminds me of the mythical *Phoenix* as they rise from the ashes of their early lives. Their courage rewards them with a rare vulnerability that sets them apart from their still broken brothers. Now, healed and authentic, even their faces change. Their facial muscles shift from tense to relaxed. They smile often and easily, and their eyes are soft and clear enough to reflect the light in their souls. Many of these brave men rekindle their artistic gifts to safely express their healing. Many offer themselves in service to others who still hold an empty cup in search of compassion. These very special men embrace the sensuality of life we women dream of. Bravo to their courage! They are a rare breed, indeed. Consider yourself blest if your heart is drawn to a truly deeply healed Little Boy Blue.

JOURNEY JOURNALING:

What are the 3 most important things I learned from this chapter?

How do I ensure that feeling empathy for a broken man does not overrule my well-being?

Who are the men in my life who qualify as Little Boy Blue? Why?

How will I apply this information in my search for my prince?

RECOMMENDED READS:

Ghosts From the Nursery by Robin Karr-Morse and Meredith S. Wiley.

VIOLENCE: Our Deadly Epidemic and Its Causes by James Gilligan, M.D.

LOST BOYS: Why Our Sons Turn Violent and How We Can Save Them by James Garbarino, Ph.D.

The Givers and the Takers by Bruce Feld and Chris Evatt

PART IV

WE

*Whatever Souls are Made of,
Yours and Mine are the Same*

20 *Anam Cara:*
The Truest Friend of Your Soul

If you live to be a hundred, I want to live to be one hundred minus
one day so I don't have to ever live without you.
Winnie the Pooh by A.A. Milne

He always, always is in my mind; not as a pleasure to myself,
but as my own being. He is more myself than I am.
Unknown

What's the point of being princess
if you don't get everything you want?
H.R. Lane-Smith

Our Terms:

INTIMACY: A private and personal utterance or action; a detailed
knowledge resulting from a close association or study; a quiet and
private atmosphere; a close personal relationship.

TRUST: Accepting responsibilities as a sacred trust; confidence
and reliance on fairness, truth, honor, or ability; responsibility for
taking good care of somebody; the position of someone expected
by others to behave responsibly or honorably.

SYNERGY: Two or more things functioning together to produce
a result not independently obtainable; the interaction of elements
that when combined produce a total effect that is greater than the
sum of the individual elements; the bonus that is achieved when
things work together harmoniously.

MATE: One of a pair.

SOULMATE: A person one has a strong affinity; twin flame.

ANAM CARA: Soul mate; the truest friend of your soul.

> **Marriage, ultimately, is the practice**
> **of becoming passionate friends.**
> Harville Hendrix

A Love Story

SUSAN

The day that up and coming young actor Jeff Bridges rode into Paradise Valley, Montana, in 1974, he had yet to see his name in really big lights. He had come to this remote town to film a comedy Western called *Rancho Deluxe.* Before the day was over, he was ordering coffee from *Black-Eyed Sue,* actually Susan Geston, a small town girl working her way through college as a waitress at a dude ranch.

Black-Eyed Sue earned her nickname sporting two black eyes and a broken nose from a recent car accident. Watching her, Jeff saw past those surface injuries into her stunningly beautiful face. And, as he soon learned, she was not only beautiful, she was also smart, funny, and available. If you asked him today, he would tell you what he knew then, *It was love at first sight.* For him, yes. Not so much for Ms. Geston.

It would be 35 years and three daughters later that Susan Geston Bridges would beam her love light up to the stage of the Kodak Theater as her *Darling* won the Oscar for Best Actor. She glowed with a timeless grace, so rare in the celebrity scene, as he praised her from the stage, endlessly, shamelessly.

Jeff has accumulated numerous awards for his dazzling performances over the years. And with each acceptance speech, he seizes his opportunity to praise his bride. Loving tributes to *My gorgeous wife, My main teacher, I'm looking at you, Sweetheart* flow from his lips like honey. *I'm more in love with her than ever*, he boldly tells interviewers. *Our relationship just keeps getting better and more intimate and sexier and all that stuff. You don't want to mess around with that.* Does the thought of cheating or leaving her ever come to mind? Are you kidding? Like any married couple, they've had their triumphs and traumas, but Jeff credits the fact that they clung together through some pretty serious storms that makes their love richer. Mr. and Mrs. Bridges are one of the most respected couples in Hollywood. Not surprisingly, Jeff and his brother, Beau, grew up in the light and laughter of their parents' loving Hollywood marriage.

The night Jeff accepted his Oscar for Best Actor in *Crazy Heart*, 41 million viewers glimpsed one tiny moment in their lavish love affair. How adorable he was when, in the middle of his acceptance speech, he stopped long enough to tell the cameraman *My wife. My beautiful wife. Get a shot of her!* As the world watched her face glowing on the screen, we could hear Jeff as he held the Oscar in his hand, whispering into the mike *Ohhh, man!*

On the day they met, it wasn't quite so romantic. Sitting in that booth in Montana, Jeff stole glances at her from behind a magazine, stalling while he found the courage to ask her out. When he finally did make the move, she turned him down with a definite *NO. Hollywood actor* was evidently not on her *Glass Slipper* list.

No, she, the waitress in a small town, wanted something more for her life than instant wealth and fame on a silver platter. Being the *love interest* of a celebrity didn't impress her much either. She expected much more from any man who dared to ask her to share even one evening of her life. Before saying *yes* to a date with Jeff Bridges, she took her own sweet time to answer her own question: *Is he WORTHY of Me?* (Excuse me. After writing that last sentence, I just need a moment to take a deep breath. Then, I'll need to add *Wow!* to my exhale). She might have been *just* a waitress, but deep within her soul, Susan Geston, a Montana waitress, embodied the royal presence and dignity of Elizabeth I.

> **It takes a mighty fine man to beat no man at all.**
> Ms. Anonymous

Mrs. Susan Geston Bridges, if ever there was a true *NaughtABimbeaux*, you are her. Indeed! Never having to work another day of your life was not enough. The promise of wealth when you had none was not enough. Having the attention of a handsome young actor was not enough. Living your life as Hollywood Royalty that you could have never dreamed of was not enough. Finding a prince that knew you were Queen............... OK... that was enough. (...wow).

There were just two significant differences between Susan Geston and Elizabeth I. Number 1, their SOCIAL STATUS: One was born into the Royal Line of England; the other had to work for every dime she owned. Number 2, their SOCIAL CIRCLE: One had the Princes of Europe begging for her hand in marriage; one had cowboys waiting for her hand to pour their coffee. Those two differences pale in comparison to what these two women, living on opposite sides of the earth, and in radically different eras, shared in common ~ expecting RESPECT as Queen.

> **As Woman**
> *I vow to marry myself ~ first.*
> *I promise to love, honor and respect me for all time.*
> *I promise to speak my truth and listen to my sacred heart.*
> *I know that I am Queen.*
> Audrey Hope

Within these last chapters, you have examined romantic relationship in its entire unconscious, ill-fated, psyche-wounding, train wreck possibilities. As you read those heart-wrenching stories, their themes brought up raw emotions of those times when your own body and soul suffered the pain of *toxic love.* For many of you, revisiting your pain was only one half of your regret. The other half came when you realized how those relationships detoured you from the path that would lead you to the one you truly seek.

The wound is the place where the Light enters you.
Rumi

Now, the circumstances of your life have brought you through and to this point of light. You have courageously bid *goodbye* to what harmed you. With your other *NaughtABimbeaux* sisters, you share the knowledge and maturity to distinguish real love from your fairy tale fantasies. From here forward, you bypass the mediocre and madness for the magic of finding a man who can and will love you. Most importantly, you have learned that to recognize *him,* you continually embrace you… Whole, complete, magnificent You ~ the Queen.

The most courageous act is still to think for yourself. Aloud.
Coco Chanel

In Chapter 1, the promise of your journey from bimbo to *NaughtABimbeaux* was to replace:

Wishes with **WISDOM**	Terror with **TRUST**
Desperation with **DIGNITY**	Panic with **POWER**

- ☑ Have your little girl wishes turned into a woman's wisdom?
- ☑ Has your paralyzing fear of failure transformed into "World, here I am!"?
- ☑ Where once you whispered in desperation, *Will he like me?* do you now debate within your deep place … **Is he WORTHY of Me?**

OK! How great does it feel to know the days of *I'm worthless without a man* are far behind you? GREAT!
So, now you stand at the center of your own universe. Really GREAT!
So… now what?

What you seek is seeking you.
Rumi

So, go live your life! It belongs to you, after all! Use your *On a Clear Day* clarity to discover what you love and do it because you love you! If you love running, or dancing, or singing, or wine tasting, enjoy! Enroll in that photography class, volunteer in your community, learn to play chess, become a Big Sister, or take up tennis! Maybe you'll even write a book. I did. You are no longer a woman desperate to have a man. You are a woman who cherishes all that she is. It's up to you now to choose what you want to do to please yourself.

As you embrace your life on your terms, your confidence will captivate everyone around you. So, do what you love. Your world will take notice. If by fate, luck, or kismet, a potential prince happens to be watching, believe me, he'll be watching! After all, a confident woman doing what she loves is beautiful to behold, right? And, if there's a possibility that he might be a real possibility, you know how to keep your heart safe while you discover *Is he fraud* or *Is he Forever?*

We always marry someone for the purpose
of finishing our childhood.
Harville Hendrix

You will analyze his writing. You will test his truth over time and in every way. You will watch him with your intuition fully engaged, and if your tummy sends you the signal *Red Flag,* you will trust it. You will learn and then test his core values to see if you are both walking in the same direction and with the same intention for your lives. You will take your sweet time because this is how you learn if he's the man who will gather you up in all your complexities and quirkiness, and still love you madly. So, do what you love. Chances are high that if he is your true soul mate, what you love doing he loves doing and that's how you will find each other. How very convenient! Then, together you will find the treasure you have both been searching for all of your lives…the *Something More* of …

ANAM CARA

Love is not finding someone you can live with.
Rather, love is finding the one you can't live without.
Anonymous

Anam Cara is one of the oldest and most beloved Celtic traditions. It is the one rare awakening between two people, as if an ancient affinity that has been latent comes awake and comes alive with the other. This deepest of loves cannot be broken by time or space or anything else. Within the other, each finds their mother and father, brother and sister, friend and beloved. Anam Cara answers the incredible spiritual hunger that lies unanswered within every one of us ~ to know and to be known. For Anam Cara lovers, a wedding is simply a celebration of the marriage that has already joined their two hearts. Anam Cara lasts for the rest of time.

If I could reach up and hold a star for every time
you've made me smile, the entire evening sky would be
in the palm of my hand.
Unknown

The Anam Cara love shared by Jeff and Sue Bridges is like watching magic happen. After all, their story does include the magic of Hollywood. To bring you back down to reality ~ that place where we all live, including Mr. and Mrs. Bridges ~ the following stories don't include Hollywood, but they do share the same magic, and everyone is just as true.

There is the wife of 18 years whose eyes get misty when her hubby leaves for a business trip of three or four days. *I thought that this would get easier, not harder after all these years. I'm so busy with the kids and the house you'd think I wouldn't miss him. Seems silly, doesn't it, that I miss him so much when he's gone from us for such a short time?*

There is the respected surgeon nearing retirement, who shares confidentially with his friend, *I've been married over 40 years, and y'know... Everything just keeps getting sweeter, even our love making becomes sweeter each time. My desire to lie in her arms has only grown through the years.*

Anam Cara brings both to that most sacred place
within each other...Home.
John O'Donahue, Irish poet

There is the widow who speaks of her buried husband in the present tense. If you ask why, she tells you, *Because death did not kill him. We are closer than ever. His clothes, still full of his scent, hang next to mine in our closet, just like always.*

There is the husband who for ten years cleared phlegm from the throat of his beloved, cancer-ridden wife. *No one loved her like I did, so I was the one who needed to take care of her.*

Love is not a feeling. Love is an action, an activity.
Genuine love implies commitment and the exercise of wisdom.
Love is the will to extend oneself for the purpose of nurturing
one's own or another's spiritual growth.
J. Scott Peck, *The Road Less Traveled*

My friend's grandparents were married 66 years. Every evening, Grandpa would fold his Darling's arm over his, and together they walked arm-in-arm down the hallway to their bedroom.

When asked by a granddaughter how old were they when they stopped making love, without hesitation, Grandma replied *Why would we stop?*

Before you were born I knew you. You grew like an unborn child beneath my heart. Every bone and plane in your body is fitted exactly with mine; every breath you take fills my lungs with air so new that the whole world gleams. Until I knew you, I never knew myself.
Margaret Renkl, *The Marigold Poems*

Your Anam Cara is the lover you endured this journey to find. He is the one **Worthy** of you. So, turning towards your North Star, allow all the richness of your journey to validate the *rightness* of the emotional intimacy you long for. Again, finding him requires your time, testing and tenacity. Most of all, it requires that you be wary and wise to ensure you find the man your heart truly longs for. He will be the man who listens and learns from you. He will be the one who looks you in the eyes, and soothes you with an uncommon ease. You will have proven to yourself, over and over and over again, that you can trust him with your truth and your tears. Without a shadow of a doubt, you will know that he is the one who will keep your soul safe and lift your heart higher and dream your dreams forward. It is his hand you know belongs in yours. And, you will not be surprised when he finds you doing what you love doing what he loves.

> ***Lovers don't finally meet.***
> ***They've been in each other all along.***
> Rumi

Blessings on your way, dear sister,

Morgan

May Nothing Evil Cross This Door
by Louis Untermeyer

May nothing evil cross this door, and may ill fortune never pry about these windows. May the roar and rain go by.

By faith made strong, the rafters will withstand the battering of the storm. This hearth, though all the world grow chill, will keep you warm.

Peace shall walk softly through these rooms, touching our lips with holy wine, till every casual corner blooms into a shrine.

With laughter drown the raucous shout, and, though these sheltering walls are thin, may they be strong to keep hate out and hold love in.

On Becoming NaughtABimbeaux

About the Author

Morgan Rose, a once certifiable bimbo, is highly qualified to write this book as a now mental health professional, researcher, educator, activist, 2 x cancer survivor, *Who's Who of American Women* recipient, and woman who knows, all too well, what is at stake when a woman sells her soul to claim a faux prince.

In her careers as a relationship expert and district psychologist, Morgan has witnessed the life-long effects of stress-filled relationships on children, adults, couples and families. Such stress risks not only emotional vulnerability, but compromises physical and mental health with wounds that often last a lifetime. With her profound respect for the integrity, intelligence and vulnerability of women seeking conscious relationship, Morgan has woven her own personal journey with years of compulsive research into the soul, science, and social trends of intimacy to give women a book that matters.

A fierce advocate for women's empowerment through higher education, Morgan has earned her Bachelor and Master degrees in psychology. She continues post-graduate research in human development and gender studies, with emphasis on the link between early bonding and adult intimacy.

Morgan has been recognized for her advocacy for human rights and social justice, and has presented to state legislatures, guest lectured at universities, and was invited by Congresswoman Lynn Woolsey to present in Washington D.C. in the areas of children, family and culture. Since 2001, she has served as Founder and Executive Director of The America's Angel Campaign.

Mission Statement of

The AMERICA'S ANGEL Campaign:

To establish the well-being of America's children
as our nation's highest priority,
ensuring their birthright to be safe and nurtured
in their own homes and homeland.

A portion of the profits from *On Becoming NaughtABimbeaux* will be donated to The America's Angel Campaign.

www.AmericasAngel.org
www.facebook.com/AmericasAngel

It's about FAMILY
It's about FUTURE
It's about TIME

BREAD for the JOURNEY

The following exercises and resources strengthen self-awareness. They have proved invaluable to other women, including many of your sisters whose stories are shared in this book. I encourage you to choose at least one, hopefully more, to support you in your own journey towards wholeness.

Your Child's Journal:

Childhood issues can tether your journey more powerfully than anything else you experience later in life. Keeping your Child's Journal provides you a path for revisiting the memories of that vulnerable time. Journal your childhood memories when you can create a quiet, spacious window of time, with no possibility of interruption. Close your door and your mind to everything that keeps you from focusing on you and your memories. This is your time to be with the one who lives in the shadow of your life.

Welcome her as if you had invited her to simply spend the afternoon. She may have much or little to tell. Deep emotion may surface or not. Nevertheless, she will come, carrying at least one memory you both intimately share. Be with her, with no judgment, no expectation, and no fear. The two of you are in no danger. You are safe and each cares for the other. Assure her that whenever she needs you, you will welcome her.

There will come a time to pick up your pen and journal the memory. Write as you would have written it then, in the voice and understanding you had at the time. Describe the situation, the environment, the face, the voice, the words said or what you wished had been said. What were you hoping for? What was provided? What was your response? What were your authentic feelings in the moment, and later on? What emotions are you feeling about it all now, as a woman on her path? When you feel complete, as if both of you have had your say, thank her for her gift. Assure her you have always loved her, and always will.

Some of us keep our Child's Journal near our childhood photo. As we write, we see ourselves in her. This brings honesty to our memories.

Dream Journal:

Dreams are your window into your hidden self, thus they provide you a treasure of insights into your truth, past, present and future. By keeping your dream journal by your bed, when you wake you can record your dreams fresh, and in as much detail and emotion as possible. Even if you recall only a few details, even if it's in the middle of the night, write down the words, the people, the action, or emotions you remember. The act of writing will improve your dream recall over time.

As your dreams reveal truth, you can trust that whatever appears, even in the form of a nightmare, is real and worthy of your attention. In time, you will likely begin to notice trends or themes in your dreams, as well. Because you have been journaling, you are more likely to notice these trends and sense their relevance to your journey. Dreams release information that benefits your psychological, emotional, mental, spiritual and physical health. As you trust them, these benefits will increase your sense of worth and power.

For information on how to interpret the meanings of your dreams, the following books are recommended:

Healing Dreams: How to Interpret Your Dreams and Change Your Life by Sarah Denning

The Dream Dictionary by Tony Crisp

The Kin of Ata are Waiting for You by Dorothy Bryant

NON-VERBAL THERAPIES

The following therapies ~ Sand Tray, Art and Dance Therapies ~ allow you to bypass your thinking brain so your feeling brain, the center of your intuition, can express itself safely. Individually, and in combination, these therapies have been used to address:

- Post-traumatic stress disorder

- Depression

- Grief, Loss, Separation Anxiety

- Anxiety and Stress

- Eating disorders

- Relationship issues

- Decision-making

- Confidence, Identity, or self-esteem issues

Art Therapy:

Creative expression allows you the opportunity to gently express your deepest knowing. Drawing, painting, sculpting, writing and composing music can help you reconcile inner conflicts, release deeply repressed emotions, foster self-awareness and personal growth. Art therapy can be done through a formal setting (such as a therapeutic art class) or informally, such as in the privacy of your home or out in nature.

American Art Therapy Association, Inc. www.arttherapy.org

Dance Therapy:

Some people find that their spirits soar when they let their feet fly. The underlying premise to dance therapy is that movement with music supports a person to safely integrate the emotional, physical, and cognitive facets of their childhood.

Formal *couple* dancing, such as ballroom, country-western, contra, square, and Latin develops the *give and take* skills so necessary in intimate relationships. You can safely learn a lot about a man by *feeling* how he leads his partner.

Sandplay Therapy:

Sandplay therapy is less traumatic than traditional talking therapies, as it is symbolic and non-invasive. A Sandplay therapist provides a safe, protected and respectful space for healing to occur. During Sandplay therapy, you view your situation from many perspectives, naturally and easily.

Sandplay is rather like a waking dream where pain, anger, fear, confusion, or conflicts are worked through on an intuitive level, rather than through monologue or dialogue. The Sandplay therapist follows you through your process until there is a feeling of release and empowerment. Association of Sandplay Therapists www.sandplay.org

Private Therapy:

Find a therapist trained in your issues and committed to your empowerment. Therapists who dictate what they think you *should* do rather than encourage you to TRUST your own wisdom can derail your journey's progress. Many therapists offer a sliding-scale fee schedule for those with financial limitations.

Massage Therapy:

Suppressed emotions are often held within our muscles and can lead to depression and disease. Massage and other forms of bodywork release these stored emotions by relaxing the body to release toxic stress, and restore well-being.

Yoga:

Yoga allows you to concentrate on your breath and relax your body. Many women find it a powerful, yet comforting tool for centering themselves in their own power of being.

Ritual:

Personal rituals can be done as often as you choose. Perhaps your ritual commemorates a significant date, season, or occasion that holds meaning for you. Or, you may want to allow openness for when your intuition says *This would be a good time*. The power of ritual is that it gives you a gentle, yet powerful tool to honor your journey from childhood forward into now and beyond.

Example: Write a letter to a parent or sibling, expressing all the things you wanted, but were too afraid to express as a child. Be as honest as if you were under oath. Be as angry, resentful, frightened or as sad as you need to be. Say as much as you need to say. Put the letter away for a day, week, or more. Then, when you choose, reread it. Are there other details you remember?

When you feel your letter is complete, decide what you want to do with it. Some women choose to keep their letter in a private place. If you are in a women's group or in private therapy, you may want to share the letter in that context. Many women go to nature. There they may tear the letter to pieces, burn it, then bury the ashes in the earth, sand, or water.

Martial Arts:

Eastern martial arts, such as Aikido and Tai Chi have supported those who are recovering from physical, sexual, or emotional abuse. You may find these techniques especially helpful for gaining a sense of ease with your own body.

Sensory Exploration:

Explore your five senses. Touch, smell, see, taste, listen, and *feel* your environment as you walk in the park, wash the dishes, enter a room, or lay in your bed. Meditating on your sensory awareness is a very gentle process that holds the potential to open you to yourself and the world around you.

NOTES:

_____

_____

_____

_____

_____

_____

_____

_____

_____

_____

_____

_____

_____

_____

_____

_____

Made in the USA
Columbia, SC
03 October 2017